Northern Roots

who we are
where we came from
and why we speak the way we do

David Simpson

© David Simpson

ISBN 1 901888 35 5 ✓

First published 2002
Reprinted 2005

Cover Design Dominic Edmunds

Published in Great Britain by
Business Education Publishers Limited
The Teleport
Doxford International
Sunderland
SR3 3XD

Tel: 0191 5252410
Fax: 0191 5201815

British Cataloguing-in-Publications Data
A catalogue record for this book is available from the British Library

Printed in Great Britain by Athenaeum Press, Gateshead.

Biography

David Simpson was born in 1967 and has been a researcher and columnist with The Northern Echo newspaper since 1994. He is the author of nine books on Northern English history including *The Millennium History of North East England* hailed by the Prime Minister, Tony Blair in his 'Millennium Address to the Nation' 1999. David lives in Durham with his wife, Abi and two cats. He is well known as a public speaker and has made numerous appearances on television and radio.

Preface

The people of Northern England are a breed apart.

Northerners speak with distinct local dialects and have their very own sense of history. In the guise of Yorkshiremen, Cumbrians, Geordies, Scousers, Lancastrians or Northumbrians, all have contributed to the rich culture of Britain.

But who are these Northerners and where did they come from?

What clues exist in history to the ancient and more recent origins of Northerners and their speech?

This book traces the languages and origins of various people who have settled in the North over two thousand years to give it the distinct character it has today.

For Abi

Contents

Introduction:
Two Thousand Years of Northerners

The First 1000 Years

If you travelled back two thousand years to live in Northern England at the start of the first millennium, one of the first things you would have to do is learn to speak Welsh. English speakers didn't exist in Britain in those days.

Even if you travelled forward another three centuries to 300 AD, you would still find that the natives spoke an old form of Welsh. You would find the North occupied by Roman soldiers, who spoke many different European languages. The Romans and some of the natives would also speak Latin, a language known to almost everyone in the Roman Empire. If you don't speak Welsh and you didn't learn Latin at school, you would have great difficulty understanding the people of the North in 300 AD.

I was only Axing

When a man from North East England axes something, it could well be a question. The word Axe is a local dialect word meaning 'to ask' and comes from the Anglo-Saxon word Acsian.

Travel forward another three centuries to 600 AD and the Romans had left Britain. You would find the Old Welsh language still spoken in some remote parts of Britain, but most people in England would speak an old Germanic language resembling Dutch or perhaps Scandinavian. It was a language that sounded vaguely English. In fact some of the words would look as if they belonged to a northern British dialect like Geordie, Yorkshire or Scots.

Viking Tykes

Yorkshiremen are sometimes known as Tykes. This is a word of Viking origin and means 'snarling dog' The name probably refers to a tough, not to be messed with attitude.

The Yorkshire Ridings

The Vikings divided Yorkshire into three parts for administrative and military purposes. These were called 'thridings' meaning 'three parts'. They were later known as 'Ridings'. The North Riding, West Riding and East Riding were official counties of Yorkshire right up until the local government reorganisation of the 1970s.

The Germanic language spoken in England in 600 AD is called Old English. It was the language of the Anglo-Saxons who had invaded our Welsh-speaking land. By 600 AD, Anglo-Saxon settlements were everywhere in England and most places were given Anglo-Saxon names.

Lets travel forward another 300 years to 900 AD. We would find an unmistakable Scandinavian influence in the northern language. This was especially apparent in Yorkshire and Cumbria, where there was significant Viking settlement. Viking words and forms of speech were very common in the North at this time and they would come to be used in all parts of Britain, including the south.

In 900 AD people of Viking origin were especially common in the north, although many could also be found in the east midlands. Scandinavian names like Olaf and Eric would be quite popular at this time, perhaps even amongst people who were not of Scandinavian origin. Irish names were popular since Irish-Vikings from the great Viking colony at Dublin could also be found throughout the North.

Viking place-names could be found almost everywhere in the north of England - as indeed they still can today. At places like York, people of Danish and Norwegian origin lived side by side with Anglo-Saxons and Celts. But could the people of northern England in 900 AD understand the English as we know it today? Well, no, not really, but more familiar English words were used in 900 AD than were used in 600 AD.

The Dragon's Place

The place names Ormskirk near Liverpool and Ormesby near Middlesbrough include the Viking name Orm meaning 'dragon'. Orm was a popular first name amongst the Vikings. Ormesby means the farm belonging to Orm', Ormskirk was the 'church belonging to Orm'.

On the whole, the language of 900 AD was still not recognisably English, so if you were able to visit northern England in 900 AD, you might need to take a Scandinavian friend to translate. Of course even they would struggle, as all languages change considerably over long periods of time. For added support you could take a person who speaks fluent Cumbrian or the Yorkshire dialect.

The Second Millennium

Leaving the Viking age behind, we can travel forward 300 years to the second millennium and the year 1200. Not surprisingly, the speech of northern England had changed once more. Some aspects of the language of 600 or 900 AD survived, but many words of Norman-French origin had been introduced and the structure of the language had changed forever.

French Bullets

The Geordie word 'Bullet' meaning a sweet is of old French origin, deriving from 'Boullette'. The word 'Bonny', used in Scottish and northern dialects derives from the French word 'Bon' meaning good.

Despite the French influence, the English of 1200 wouldn't seem quite so foreign as that of 900 or 600 AD. It seemed to have a much closer resemblance to the English of today. This was because French had a major influence on the development of the English language. If you have ever read the works of Chaucer you might be able to understand the English speech of 1200, but you would need to take a student of medieval English to help you translate.

Even with this help, you might still have a problem in the north of England, where distinct dialects were spoken. This would make communication a bit more difficult, even for the Chaucer experts.

You could try speaking to some of the barons or earls that had so much power at this period of time. They tended to speak an old form of French, rather than English. This was because the barons were largely descendants of the Norman conquerors who had arrived in 1066. Unfortunately, if you can't speak French and you have never read Chaucer, then perhaps 1200 would not be for you.

Shakespeare's Time

At the end of the Norman period it was possible to look back over a thousand years and conclude that northerners were composed of a wide mixture of people. Britons, Anglo-Saxons, Vikings, Irish and Scots had already contributed to the northern stock and a northern identity and dialect was already apparent. The Norman Conquest would be the last military invasion of our shores from overseas, but northerners and their language continued to evolve.

If we were to set off once again on our time travelling journey to the year 1600, the language of England would seem more familiar to our modern ears - "Wilt thou journey to 1600? Thou know'st the language of this age, why 'tis Shakespeare" - well in the north it was not quite the same as Shakespeare, but it was similar. Up in the north in 1600, imagine a Shakespearean type of language spoken with a heavy local dialect. Of course not everyone was as well-educated, articulate or as poetically talented as Shakespeare.

We can assume that the speech of the rougher, poorer people had a more limited vocabulary in Shakespeare's time. The use of older dialect words of Anglo-Saxon or Scandinavian origin would have been more widespread among the people of the north and this was especially the case in rural areas. In wealthy merchant towns like Newcastle , the dialect was probably less evident than it was in the rural areas and perhaps less evident than it is today. However, over time people from surrounding rural areas sought work in the towns. The people from these rural areas were often rough, uneducated and many spoke what we would have found to be an impenetrable dialect.

The Border Reivers, the people of the Border regions of Northumberland and Scotland had a particularly rough reputation in 1600. They shared a common way of life and a very similar dialect. The Border people saw little influence from outside. Many English people feared travelling into the North Country beyond the Tyne. In fact travelling north of the Tees in those days was seen as a dangerous journey.

So even if you think you might be able to understand the language of Shakespeare – as spoken in a rough northern dialect - you might still prefer not to visit the far north of England in the year 1600. But if you do, watch out for those Border Reivers!

Northerners 1800-2000

Up until the 1700s the population of the north was mainly rural, but by 1800 things began to change in a major way. In the eighteenth and nineteenth century heavy industry grew at a rapid pace. Northern towns expanded well beyond their original boundaries, attracting thousands of people, not just from the rural localities, but from all corners of England, Scotland and Wales. Many towns expanded from populations of a few hundred or a few thousand to populations of more than one hundred thousand.

One of the major influxes of population in the North came from Ireland, particularly after the potato famine in 1845. The North of England was a major destination for the Irish and they made up a very significant proportion of the north's population, particularly in the large cities of North West England like Liverpool and Manchester. In parts of the north, like the mining towns and villages of Durham and Yorkshire, new people could make up more than half the population. Their children would quickly adopt the local dialects of the region or locality as they moved from village to village to seek work.

In the twentieth century the great melting pot of northern people continued to grow. Cultures from as far apart as Asia and the Caribbean made significant contributions to this cultural mix, especially in the larger cities. If you were able to visit the North of England in 1850 or 1950, you might have a better chance of communicating with the people of the North than you would have done in 1200 or 600 AD. None the less, you would still be able to find a great variety of accents, dialects, languages and ethnic types.

Searching for Ancient Roots

As we look back over two thousand years of our northern history we can see that our northern roots have many different origins. The language and way of life has changed many times over the centuries, but surprisingly even today, we find much evidence in tracing the roots of our northern origins through place-names, dialects, surnames, traditions, folklore, archaeology and even in the colour of our eyes and hair.

Sadly some of the evidence for our ancient roots is being eroded away. Partly through the influence of television and mass media our dialects are being watered down and some may be lost forever. Local variations in speech are now less evident than they were even a few decades ago. In many cases only a few dialect words survive and sometimes in localities where they weren't originally used. As older dialect speakers pass away, the old dialects pass with them, making the study of dialect of great importance in this day and age.

The gradual erosion of our northern dialects is a sad loss, but our links with the people of the past are not entirely severed. Modern technology has enabled us to unearth new clues to our origins in some quite surprising ways. Improvements in archaeological study and genetic research have allowed us to find new links with the past. Today it is possible to tell if a man is descended from a Norwegian Viking simply by taking a sample scraping of DNA from his tongue.

Using computer technology it is also possible to recreate the face of an ancient ancestor from a skull found in an archaeological dig. So we can look a Northern Viking or an ancient Celt straight in the face and wonder if he or she might be one of our ancestors.

Northerners – A Breed Apart?

Today 'Northerners' are a breed apart. Yorkshiremen, Northumbrians, Cumbrians, Geordies, Lancastrians, Scousers and Mancunians all have distinct northern cultures, dialects and traditions that are a product of their history. All of these cultures are different in their own way. Some may have developed in ancient times, while some will be recent. Some will be such a tantalising mixture of both that it is often impossible to tell where their origins lie, but everywhere there are clues.

So who are the people of the North? Where did we come from? Why do we speak the way we do?

This book will follow the course of northern history over two thousand years and attempt to answer some of these fascinating questions.

Northern England's counties and regions

For the purposes of this book the north of England covers the historic counties of Yorkshire, Lancashire, Northumberland, Durham, Cumberland, Westmorland and Cheshire. These counties trace their origins back to ancient and medieval times, but their boundaries have changed considerably in recent decades to represent the populations of the larger urban regions and cities.

Many of the boundary changes took place in the early 1970s when 'metropolitan' counties were created in the most populous regions. These were followed by further boundary changes during the 1990s. Many of the most populous towns and boroughs in the north are now counties in their own right. This book is primarily concerned with the historic counties rather than administrative units of local government.

Nevertheless, many of the larger cities, like Newcastle and Liverpool have strong local identities and have an important place in this book, particularly in our quest to find the diverse origins of people in the north.

The North of England can be divided into three distinct regions. Sometimes there is a difference in opinion as to where the regional boundaries should lie and administrators do not necessarily observe tradition when drawing up boundaries. For example the now defunct County of Humberside, created in the 1970s combined land from the East Riding of Yorkshire with land in northern Lincolnshire, even though Lincolnshire was historically and culturally part of the midlands.

The three main regions of Northern England are Yorkshire, North Eastern England and North Western England. The former Lake District counties of Cumberland and Westmorland are now known as Cumbria and in this book are included with the North West region.

North West England and its Population

The North West is by far the most populous region in the north of England. Most of this population is concentrated in the south of the region around Manchester and Liverpool and to some extent this densely populated region continues southward into the western midlands towards Birmingham and westwards across the Pennines towards Leeds in Yorkshire. By contrast, Cumbria in the far north of the region is a sparsely populated county.

The North West includes the historic counties of Lancashire, Cheshire, Cumberland and Westmorland with most of the population concentrated in the old textile towns of southern Lancashire. However, Lancashire is now only a shadow of its former self. Populous places like Manchester, Bolton, Bury, Oldham, Salford, Wigan, Liverpool, St Helens, Blackburn, and Warrington that were once part of Lancashire are now counties in their own right.

North West Population

In the year 2000, the population of the North West was **6,893,900**. This can be broken up into:

Greater Manchester: 2,585,700
Liverpool and Merseyside: 1,403,400
Lancashire: 1,140,700
Other boroughs: 600,400
Cheshire: 672,700
Cumbria: 491,000

Yorkshire and its Population

Yorkshire was historically comprised of the East, West and North Ridings of Yorkshire and for much of its history formed the most populous region of the north. In the industrial age its population became concentrated in expanding textile towns like Leeds and Bradford and in other industrial cities like Sheffield. Today most of Yorkshire's population is concentrated in the far south west of the region.

Yorkshire Population

In the year 2000, the population of the Yorkshire region was **4,750,000**. This can be broken up as follows:

Hull and East Yorkshire: 573,200
North Yorkshire: 574,600
York: 179,300
South Yorkshire: 1,301,500
West Yorkshire: 2,121,400

The North East and its Population

The North East is the smallest of the three main northern regions. Its population is concentrated in the urban regions in and around the lower reaches of the Rivers Tyne, Wear and Tees, each associated with the major cities and towns of Newcastle, Sunderland and Middlesbrough. Much of County Durham surrounds these three major urban regions and is dominated by former coal mining settlements. The County of Northumberland to the north of Tyne is largely rural and lies close to the border with Scotland. It is one of the most sparsely populated parts of the north.

North East Population

In the year 2000, the population of the North East was **2,577,400**. This can be broken up as follows:

Tyneside and Wearside: 1,103,600
Teesside and Darlington: 657,300
County Durham: 506,100
Northumberland: 310,400

Part One:
Tribal Origins

*Bronze mask from the Brigantian tribal stronghold of Stanwick
near Scotch Corner, North Yorkshire*

Part One:
Tribal Origins

Tribal Beginnings

The Local and regional cultures of Britain, like those found in the north of England are sometimes referred to as 'tribal'. It is a tribalism that might be expressed in the team colours that we wear or perhaps in the local dialects that we speak. In our well-ordered and often confusing society, this sense of tribalism may give us a link to the past and a feeling of belonging to a community or a distinct cultural group.

Tribalism is a deeply rooted feature of the human psyche and is certainly an ancient feature of Britain's heritage. If we go back to the beginning of the first Millennium, to the age of the Celts, Britain was divided into several tribes who all spoke a form of Welsh. The tribes lived in hill forts, in well-defined regions and were often at war with each other.

Although these tribes have left no written records of their history, they were well-organised warriors and fine craftsmen, skilled in the manufacture of iron weapons. They were artistically advanced, creating precious jewellery and ornate goods and were very knowledgeable farmers. The Celts of Britain are particularly remembered for their fearless reputation on the battlefield and for their mastery of the chariot, but they were no contest for the military technology and organisation of the Romans. When the Romans invaded Britain in 43 AD the Celtic tribesmen were defeated one by one. Only in the difficult highland terrain of Caledonia would the Romans fail to subdue the native tribes. Ireland was also left untouched by the Roman invasion.

Who were the Celts?

The Celts developed from Bronze Age and Iron Age cultures that emerged in the upper River Danube region of what is now Austria and southern Germany in the period from 1000 to 500 BC. Celts were famed for their continuous raiding and settlement of neighbouring regions, for their iron making and horse riding skills and for their gradual domination of central Europe. The Celts were a tribal people living in fortified villages and each tribe had its own chieftain.

The Celtic religious practices were strongly influenced by nature and were administered by a knowledgeable, well-organised priestly class of men called druids. As a people, the Celts were often described as fair-haired or more typically red-haired. The Greeks and Romans described them as tall, muscular and light-skinned, but this is now thought to be a description of the Celtic warrior classes that were perhaps of northern, Germanic origin.

The term Celtic is more reliably used for the description of a particular cultural group or a group of languages than as a description of a physical type. In most of Europe the Celts were gradually absorbed over many centuries into the populations of many different tribes and nations, but a small number of Celtic languages survive in certain localities to this day. Most of these are in Britain.

Celtic languages

Celtic languages were once spoken across the whole of Europe. They included Celtiberian spoken in Spain, Gaulish spoken in France, Galatian spoken in Turkey and Lepontic spoken in parts of Italy and Switzerland. These languages died out many, many centuries ago but certain Celtic languages known as 'Insular Celtic' survived on the fringe of Europe in the British Isles and neighbouring Brittany. The Celtic languages of this part of Europe can be divided into two distinct categories , simplistically described as 'British' and 'Gaelic'.

'British' Celtic languages, are also known as 'Brythonic' and include modern Welsh, as well as the ancient Welsh of the Britons, the Cornish language spoken in Cornwall until the 18th century and Breton, a language still spoken in the Brittany region of France.

'Gaelic' Celtic languages also known as 'Goidelic' include the Gaelic language of Ireland, where the name is pronounced 'Gaylick' and the Gaelic language of Scotland, where the name is pronounced 'Gallic'. Gaelic languages also include Manx, the name of a Celtic language once spoken on the Isle of Man.

The origin of the Celts in Britain

The native people of Roman Britain are often described as Celts. In fact they were the descendants of many ancient peoples who had lived in the British Isles for thousands of years from the Stone Age and Bronze Age onwards. These ancient people have left their mark in enigmatic sites like the Castlerigg Stone circle in Cumbria, the Devils Arrows of Boroughbridge in Yorkshire or the mysterious cup and ring markings of Northumberland. It is thought that the descendants of these people ultimately adopted the language of the Celts, who were an Iron Age people from central Europe. The Celts did not invade and settle Britain until approximately 600 BC . It is possible that the fringe areas of Britain like Wales, Ireland and Scotland actually saw the least Celtic settlement, even though these are the areas where Celtic culture, language and place-names have survived the longest. Today all pre-Roman people of Britain are often known as 'Celts', but the 'Celts' of ancient Britain are really a mixture of many peoples, who have intermixed over thousands of years.

These enigmatic cup and ring markings on Doddington Moor, Northumberland date from the Bronze Age and so predate the Celtic settlement in Britain.

The Brigantes and other Northern Tribes

The Brigantes were the largest Welsh speaking tribe of Roman-Celtic Britain and they dominated the countryside of what we now call northern England. The Brigantes were a confederation of several smaller tribes with territory extending from southern Yorkshire to southern Northumberland. Their lands extended from the shores of the North Sea to the Irish Sea.

The name Brigantes is thought to mean 'people of the uplands' or 'the hill dwellers'. The tribe may also have taken its name from Brigit, a Celtic Deity. We know only a little about the smaller tribal groups who made up the confederation of the Brigantes but it seems probable that they were focused around the dales and river valleys that dissect the northern region. However, only a few of the Brigantes' affiliate tribes are known by name.

Hill forts associated with the Brigantes included Almondbury near Huddersfield and Stanwick near Scotch Corner in Yorkshire. Stanwick is thought to have been the capital of the Brigantian queen, Cartimandua; she was the most powerful person in the north, while her husband Venutius was a consort, not a king. However, the queen made an unpopular truce with the Romans and many of her tribesmen revolted against her. The Brigantes were eventually defeated by the Romans in a great battle at Scotch Corner in 71 AD. The Romans rescued Cartimandua but her name then disappears from history. Cartimandua has the distinction of being the first northerner mentioned in history.

Tribal Origins: Circa 150AD.

Like many other British tribal groups, the Brigantes had to accept the Romans as their masters. The Romans encouraged tribes to adopt Roman ways and one way of achieving this was through the development of Roman towns called 'civitas'. The Brigantian civitas was at Aldborough near Boroughbridge, about

fifteen miles north west of York. The Romans called it Isurium Brigantum.

The Brigantes were not the only tribe known to have lived in what is now the North of England. Other tribes mentioned in Roman times include the Carvetti who were a small tribe who lived in northern Cumbria, probably in the region of Carlisle. Further south, another tribe connected with the Brigantes was the Setantii who occupied the Fylde peninsula area on the coast of Lancashire near Blackpool. The Romans built a seaport on this coast which they called Portus Setantiorum. It was most likely located at Fleetwood on the River Wyre. In southern and western Yorkshire a tribe called the Latenses were also recorded. This tribe may have been associated with the Leeds area.

The northern area of the Brigantes territory was in southern Northumberland. Here lived the affiliate tribes called the Lopocares, Corionototae and Tectoverdi all located in and around the Tyne Valley. The Corionototae may have been associated with the area around Corbridge.

To the north of the Brigantes, in north Northumberland lived another major tribe called the Votadini, who were quite separate from the Brigantes. They were described as 'friendly to Rome' and their territory extended as far north as Edinburgh and the Firth of Forth. Like the Brigantes, the Votadini were a federation of smaller tribes but we do not know the names of their affiliate tribes. Major hill forts that possibly lay within the Votadini's domain included

Yeavering Bell near Wooler in what is now Northumberland, Eildon in the Tweed valley of what is now lowland Scotland and Traprain Law between Dunbar and Edinburgh. Many other hill forts can be found within their territory suggesting that the Votadini were often at war, perhaps with their near neighbours the Selgovae. The Selgovae territory lay slightly to the west or north of the Votadini and was possibly located in the Tweed valley. The exact boundaries of this territory are uncertain.

Paris-upon-Humber?

One of the most important tribes in northern Britain was the Parisi who lived north of the Humber in the chalk hills of the Yorkshire Wolds. The Roman Civitas or capital of the Parisi was at Brough on the banks of the Humber. The territory of the Parisi was the area we know today as East Yorkshire and was until recently part of the now defunct county of Humberside. Parisi immediately makes us think of the city of Paris and there was a possible connection. Parisi was the name of a Gaulish tribe in France and it was this continental tribe that gave its name to the city of Paris. The name of the Yorkshire Parisi suggests that east Yorkshire may have had close cultural links with the continental tribe. There were similarities in the burial practices of the British Parisi and those of the Celts in France and both buried their dead in large cemeteries. However, the Parisi of Yorkshire still had more in common with other British tribes than they had with those of the continent. We should also remember that tribal names like 'Parisi' were names given to the tribes by the Romans. We do not know the names used by the tribes themselves.

Multi-Cultural Romans

The Roman era in Britain lasted three and a half centuries. Over this long period of time the Romans certainly had some influence on the people and culture of Britain. We know that some Romans intermarried with the natives and at least some of these people must have remained in Britain after the Roman Empire collapsed. So, Northerners are partly Roman in origin. However, this would not necessarily make us part Italian. Most of the 'Romans' occupying Britain seventeen centuries ago were not actually Italian, although most could speak Latin.

Soldiers serving in Britain's Roman army came from all corners of the Empire and were from many different cultural groups. This was the case in the north and was very apparent along Hadrian's Wall in the third and fourth century. It is known for example that Germanic people like Frisians, Lingones and Batavians formed Roman military units along Hadrian's Wall at forts like Wallsend, Rudchester, Carrawburgh and Housesteads.

The presence of the Frisians in the Roman north is interesting, because the Frisian language and people were very similar to the Anglo-Saxons, a neighbouring people, who would invade Britain in the fifth and sixth centuries. The Frisian language will have seen many changes over the centuries, but it is still spoken today in parts of the Netherlands and in some areas of northern Germany. Significantly, Frisian is spoken in the German region called Schleswig-Holstein close to the border with Denmark. This was an area most closely associated with the Anglo-Saxons before they came to Britain. Frisian is the continental language that most resembles English and it has a number of features in common with northern English dialects like 'Geordie'. So some aspects of the

'Geordie' dialect may have already been in use along the Tyne in Roman times.

Germans weren't the only Europeans serving along the Roman wall. Asturians from the north west of Spain occupied the forts at Benwell and Chesters on the Tyne, while Halton Chesters, near Newcastle held a garrison of Sabinians from Pannonia in what is now Hungary. At Carvoran, near Haltwhistle, there lived a cohort of Dalmatian soldiers from what is now Serbia-Croatia. Even non-Europeans served in the Roman army. At South Shields, a unit of barge operators from the River Tigris, in what is now Iraq served at the mouth of the Tyne. At Carlisle, there was a unit of North Africans from what is now Libya.

Mancunian Mamuciums

Manchester folk are called Mancunians. The Roman name for Manchester was Mamucium meaning the 'breast-like hill'. The word Chester in place-names signifies a 'Roman fort' and was used by the later Anglo-Saxons to describe a Roman site.

Catterick Cataracts

The place-name Catterick in North Yorkshire derives from the Roman word 'Cataracta' meaning waterfall. It is probably named from its proximity to the cataracts on the nearby River Swale. The Romans called Catterick Cataractonium.

Roman Celts

Roman soldiers came from all parts of Europe, but some native Britons also enlisted in the Roman army. Strangely, perhaps for reasons of security, most Britons who joined the Roman army had to serve abroad. However, there was a unit of Britons belonging to the Cornovii tribe of Shropshire and Cheshire who served in the army at Newcastle upon Tyne's Roman fort.

The Britons were Celts and were closely related to the Gauls, a Celtic people who lived in France and Belgium. Many Gauls served in the Roman army and occupied forts like Vindolanda and Castlesteads on Hadrian's Wall. Some Gauls could also be found serving at the wall fort of Housteads.

Housteads Roman Fort, Hadrian's Wall.

Scottish 'Gallic' and the French connection

We often use the word 'Gallic' to describe something that is typically 'French'. 'Gallic' is related to the word 'Gaelic' - the name given to the native Celtic languages of Scotland and Ireland. In fact the Scots pronounce the word Gaelic as 'Gallic'. This is no coincidence and is a vestige of a common Celtic heritage. Gallic originally meant Gaulish, because the Romans called the Celts 'Gauls' or 'Galli'. Most of France and parts of neighbouring Germany were known as Gaul because of the Celtic inhabitants who lived there in Roman times. The Celtic language of Gaul was replaced by the Latin speech of the Romans and this Latin eventually developed into the French language. Most of Gaul came to be known as France after Roman times when it was conquered and settled by a Germanic people called the Franks.

Roman Civilians

The Roman occupation of Northern Britain was not entirely of a military nature. Small civilian settlements called 'vicus' developed outside Roman forts, where traders lived, alongside wives and children of Roman soldiers. Such settlements have been found at Roman forts as far north as Piercebridge in Durham and Housesteads in Northumberland. There were other places where mixed native and Roman settlements developed, quite independent of Roman forts. At Hardwick on the outskirts of Sedgefield in County Durham, a major 'Roman-British' civilian settlement of this kind was excavated in 2002. It includes the outlines of several buildings, including the remnants of a glassworks and bronze works. This kind of non-military civilian settlement is often found in the south, but it is an extremely rare find in the North East of England, where Roman civilian settlements are usually next to military bases. The settlement may have been constructed during a peaceful period.

One of the biggest and most important Roman towns in the north was of course York. Here, the massive civilian settlement was awarded the status of 'colonia' making it one of the highest-ranking Roman towns in the empire. It developed on the south side of the River Ouse opposite the great Roman Legionary fortress. Retired soldiers often lived in settlements like these and there is much evidence that women also came to Britain from foreign parts to live in these places.

Surely it is possible that some of these multi-cultural 'Romans' remained in northern Britain to intermix with the natives beyond Roman times? At least some northerners of today must be descended from the Romans.

Part Two:
When We Were Welsh

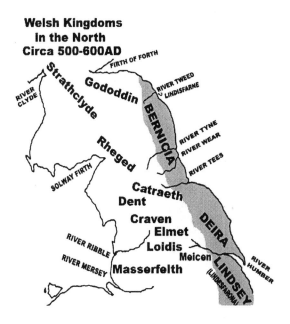

Welsh Kingdoms in the North, Circa 500 – 600 AD

Shaded area shows early Anglian Kingdoms

Part Two:
When we were Welsh

Welsh Kingdoms in Yorkshire and Lancashire

From around 400 AD, the Roman army needed to defend the city of Rome against the invading Goths. We are told that most of the Roman soldiers left Britain for good. Exactly how many, if any of the multi-cultural 'Roman' civilians remained in Britain is not known. It seems probable that many of the people who stayed in Britain were native 'Britons' who continued to speak a form of Welsh with some Latin influence.

Welsh speaking Britons established several kingdoms in the north after the Romans departed. These kingdoms were eventually seized by the invading Anglo-Saxons in the sixth and seventh centuries and were incorporated into the Kingdom of Northumbria.

It is thought that one of the Welsh kingdoms was called Catraeth. It was probably centred on the Rivers Swale and Tees, perhaps with a capital at Catterick. The history of this kingdom is uncertain. Another ancient region with a Welsh name is Craven, located in the Yorkshire Pennines. The name derives from the ancient Welsh word 'Craf' meaning Garlic, perhaps from the wild garlic that grows in the dales

of this region. Craven is now the name of a large district council centred upon the town of Skipton. The nearby region called Dent may also have formed a Celtic kingdom and is thought to derive its name from an old Celtic word for a hill.

Celtic Eccles

Place-names containing the word 'Eccles' such as Eccles near Manchester, Eccleston near St Helens, Eccleston near Chester and Ecclesfield near Sheffield have Roman-Celtic origins. They are thought to have been the sites of Christian churches that existed in Roman-Celtic times. In the later period of the Roman occupation many Romans converted to Christianity. Romans used the word 'ecclesiasticus' and this derived from a Greek word 'ekklesia' meaning 'assembly' or 'church'. Some Roman Celtic Christian sites may have survived the Anglo-Saxon invasion and are perhaps remembered in the Eccles place-names.

Northern Place-names of Celtic Origin

Cockermouth in Cumbria derives its name from the Welsh stream name 'crwca' (cocker) meaning crooked stream. The place-name Ince in Makerfield comes from the Celtic word 'Inys' meaning 'island'. Makerfield was the name of a Celtic region. Morecambe in Lancashire is Celtic and means something like 'sea bay'. Pendle Hill in Lancashire has a Celtic name like Yorkshire's Penyghent. It was once called Penne Hill meaning 'hill-hill'. Penrith in Cumbria comes from the old Welsh 'Pen Rhyd' meaning hill ford. Wigan was probably originally called Tref Wigan but this Celtic name has not been explained. Hull is a river with a Celtic name in Yorkshire that gives its name to the city of Hull, while the River Wyre in Lancashire has a Celtic name meaning 'winding stream'. The River Nidd in Yorkshire has a Celtic name that means 'shining' whilst the Ure of Wensleydale means 'holy water'.

One of the most well-recorded Welsh kingdoms in the post-Roman period was Elmet. It is still remembered in place-names like Barwick in Elmet and Sherburn in Elmet near Leeds. It is possible that Leeds was part of this Celtic Kingdom as Leeds also has a Celtic name. Leeds was known to the Celts as Leodis and was a Celtic region in its own right. The Venerable Bede mentioned Leodis in Anglo-Saxon times, but the boundaries of Leodis are uncertain. The place-names Ledston and Ledsham about ten miles east of Leeds, were probably Anglo-Saxon settlements within the old Celtic region of Leeds.

A Welsh Mountain in Yorkshire

One obvious clue to the Celtic-Welsh origin of Northern England is in place-names. In the Pennines of Yorkshire, for example, we find a remarkable survival of a Welsh name in the famous hill called Pen-y-Ghent.

This is a name that would not seem at all out of place in Wales. Indeed, if you look it up in an atlas of Britain you will find several names beginning with the words Pen-y. Strangely they are all in Wales, with the exception of Pen-y-Ghent which is in Yorkshire.

Pen is Welsh for 'top or head' and is closely related to the Scottish-Gaelic word 'Ben' as in Ben Nevis. The -y- in Pen-y-Ghent is the Welsh definite article. In other words 'y' means 'the' in Welsh. The meaning of Ghent is uncertain but it could be an ancient Celtic word 'Gaint' or 'Cant' meaning 'border'. Perhaps it was situated on the border of Celtic kingdoms lying on either side of the Pennines.

Pen-y-Ghent's name survived because the hill was so prominent and well known. In this remote upland area, the Welsh language had a better chance of surviving and this has helped the ancient name to survive over a very long period of time.

Another Welsh kingdom in Yorkshire was Meicen, known to the Anglo-

Saxons as 'Heathfield'. It covered the marshy lowland area of Hatfield Chase, near Doncaster. In the North West, the land between the River Ribble and River Mersey may have formed a Welsh kingdom called Masserfelth, later known as Makerfield and remembered in the place-name Ashton in Makerfield near Wigan.

Finally, there is one other very surprising 'Welsh' name in Yorkshire that must be mentioned. A few miles south east of Sheffield we find a place simply called Wales. It is an old name, probably of Anglo-Saxon origin but it almost certainly refers to Welsh speaking Britons who lived there in ancient times. It was not the name of a Welsh kingdom in South Yorkshire.

The Welsh of Cumberland

The nation of Wales has some of Britain's most mountainous terrain and this may help to explain why Welsh, the language of the Britons, survives there, centuries after the Anglo-Saxon conquest of England. Invaders would have found it hard to penetrate the Cambrian Mountains of Wales and this gave the native culture a much better chance of survival. The same was also true in the Cumbrian Mountains of what is now the English Lake District.

Celtic Carlisle

The place-name Carlisle is a combination of the ancient British or Welsh word 'caer' meaning 'fort' and the Roman name Luguvallium. Luguvallium means the wall of the god Lugus.

It is no coincidence that 'Cambrian' and 'Cumbrian' are similar names. 'Cumbria' derives its name from Cumberland meaning 'Cymru Land'. In other words Cumberland means 'Land of the Welsh'. 'Cymru' is the Welsh word for 'Wales' while 'Cymric' is the Welsh word for the 'Welsh'. Once we realise that Cymru is pronounced 'Cimree', it is not hard to see how 'Cimree land' became Cumberland.

Celtic River-names

Rivers often keep their ancient Welsh-Celtic names and some trace their origins back to more mysterious ancient Indo-European languages related to ancient Asian languages like Sanskrit. The name of the Humber is Celtic and means 'good-well river' but the root of this name could be traced back to the Sanskrit 'Ambhas' meaning water. Many Celtic river-names often simply mean 'water', as the ancient Celts seem to have had several words for water. The Welsh word for a river is 'Afon' and this has resulted in the English River name Avon in the south of England. In the north we find many Celtic river-names like Blyth in Northumberland, while place-names like Colne in Lancashire also derive from ancient Celtic river-names.

The Ouse in Yorkshire may just mean 'water' and could be related to the Sanskrit word 'Udso', while the River Wear in County Durham has a Celtic name meaning 'water' or perhaps 'blood river'. Tyne is an ancient Celtic river-name that occurs more than once in the British Isles and may simply mean 'river'. The name of the Tees is thought to be related to the ancient Welsh 'Tes' meaning 'sunshine and heat' and could mean 'boiling, surging water'. It could be pre-Celtic. The name of the River Ribble in Lancashire could be either Celtic or Anglo-Saxon in origin.

Cumberland was once the heartland of Rheged, a Welsh kingdom that held out against the Anglo-Saxons for some

time. A powerful king called Urien ruled Rheged. He fought against the Anglo-Saxons and one of his battles was fought on the island of Lindisfarne in the North East. Urien is sometimes thought to be a model for the legendary King Arthur.

Derwent and Darwen - the oak river

Derwent is a Celtic name meaning 'oak-river'. It is the name of a river in Yorkshire, Derbyshire and the Northumberland/Durham border. It has given rise to the name of Lake Derwentwater in Cumbria and the place-name Darwen near Blackburn in Lancashire.

Loughs, Lakes and Linns

In Northumberland and Ireland lakes are sometimes called 'Loughs'. It is an ancient Celtic word pronounced 'Loff' in the North-East and 'Loch' in Ireland. In Wales, a lake is called a 'Linn'. In Northumberland and north Durham a Linn is a waterfall, probably named from the pools formed at the foot of each fall.

It seems possible that Rheged's people were descendants of the Brigantian tribe of Roman times. Brigantian territory had certainly stretched into Cumbria, although there was a smaller tribe affiliated to the Brigantes called the Carvetti in the region of Carlisle. The Anglo-Saxon kingdom of Northumbria eventually seized Rheged, but significant Welsh speaking populations are likely to have survived in Cumberland for some time. Several Welsh place-names can still be found in Cumbria like Penrith, Blencathra and Penruddock.

When considering the possible Welsh origins of Cumbria and the North, mention should be made of the strange counting system used until recent times by shepherds in Cumbria and the Yorkshire Dales, as well as in other regions like Lincolnshire. The counting system looks Welsh in origin and uses the following numbers:

1 -- Yan

2 -- Tan

3 -- Tethera

4 -- Methera

5 -- Pimp

6 -- Sethera

7 -- Lethera

8 -- Hovera

9 -- Dovera

10 -- Dick

11 -- Yan-a-dick

12 -- Tyan-a-dick

13 -- Tethera-a-dick

14 -- Methera-a-dick

15 -- Bumfit

16 -- Yan-a-bumfit

17 -- Tyan-a-bumfit

18 -- Tethera-a-bumfit

19 -- Methera-a-bumfit

20 -- Giggot

There were numerous variations of this counting system across northern England, but all have similarities to the numbers of the Welsh language. The similarities are often closer in pronunciation than they are in spelling. For example the number five in Welsh is 'Pump' but is pronounced 'Pimp' while Ten is 'Deg' and is pronounced 'Dehg'.

The Scots of Ireland and the Welsh of Scotland

We think of Gaelic as the ancient Celtic language of Scotland but it wasn't the only Celtic language. In fact Gaelic was introduced to Caledonia by a tribe of invading people called the Scots, or to give them their full name Dal Riata Scots. The Scots came from Ireland and throughout most of the Roman period, Ireland was the only place where the Scots could be found. So, to the Romans, a Scot was an Irishman.

Specifically, the Scots came from the northern part of Hibernia - the Roman name for Ireland. Many Scots left northern Hibernia to invade and settle in Caledonia - the Roman name for Scotland. The Scots settled in the Western Isles and western shores of Caledonia in the region called Argyll that lies just to the north of the River Clyde. The language of the Scots was 'Gaelic' and would gradually replace the language, spoken by the native Caledonians who were called Picts. The language of the Picts is something of a mystery. There is a much debate as to whether the Picts spoke a Celtic language or a much older European language.

Wallace the Welsh

Welsh speaking Britons made up a significant proportion of southern Scotland's population in early times, especially in the south west. One interesting Scottish link with the Welsh is the Scottish surname Wallace. The name means 'Welshman' or 'Briton'. It is likely that the first person to be called Wallace was a Briton from south western Scotland.

In the Lowlands of Caledonia, to the south of the Rivers Forth and Clyde, the native people were not Picts but were Britons who spoke Welsh. Or at least they did until the Anglo-Saxons arrived. The Welsh-speaking people of the eastern lowland region around Edinburgh belonged to a tribe of Britons called the Gododdin. The Gododdin were probably descendants of the tribe known to the Romans as the Votadini. Edinburgh Castle stands on the site of a fortress that belonged to both the Gododdin and the Votadini. The Britons living in this Welsh speaking region were eventually subdued by the invading Anglo-Saxons whose Kingdom of Northumbria stretched as far north as the Firth of Forth.

Bishop Auckland's Clyde connection

The town of Bishop Auckland in the English County of Durham is situated within a district that was once known as Aucklandshire. It is thought to have Celtic origins. Early spellings of the name Auckland show that Auckland was originally called 'Alcluith'. Strangely, this is the old name for Dumbarton, the ancient capital of Strathclyde. Perhaps the Welsh kingdom of Stratchlyde stretched as far south as Bishop Auckland.

Another possibility is that this is purely a coincidence. Perhaps Clyde was simply the old name for the River Gaunless at Bishop Auckland, since the name Gaunless only goes back to Viking times and the earlier name for the River is not known. Bishop Auckland stands on a hill overlooking the Gaunless and is the site of a castle owned by the Bishops of Durham.

The Britons of south west Scotland held out against the Anglo-Saxons for much longer than the Gododdin were able to do in the east. In south west Scotland, the Welsh speaking kingdom called Strathclyde survived for some time. At its peak, Strathclyde stretched from the River Clyde to as far south as Cumbria and thus included Rheged.

The capital of Strathclyde was situated on a massive fortified rock overlooking the estuary of the Clyde. This was Dumbarton rock, named 'Alcluith' by the Britons. The name means 'rock of the Clyde' and can still be seen in Dumbarton today. Interestingly, Dumbarton derives its name from Dun Breatann meaning 'fortress of the Britons'. The site was besieged and taken by the Picts and Northumbrians in 756 AD. Strathclyde became part of Scotland in the eleventh century, so Welsh is of course no longer spoken there today.

The Welsh were 'Foreign'

The Romans abandoned Britain around 400 AD, leaving it virtually defenceless. Britons and any others who remained were at the mercy of the raiding Picts and the newly invading Scots. For protection, the Britons searched for mercenaries to help defend their land and sought the help of the Anglo-Saxons. Anglo-Saxons were a Germanic group of people closely related to the Frisians. Some had served as mercenaries in the Roman army. They were tough, experienced fighters willing to fight in return for reward.

At first the employment of Anglo-Saxons was probably a success, but in the long run it proved to be a disaster for the native Britons. Anglo-Saxons seized British land for themselves and launched a full-scale military invasion of our shores. They gradually established their own kingdoms in Britain and showed contempt for the native Britons who they called 'Waelisc' - meaning 'foreigner or slave'.

21

'Waelisc 'is the origin of the words 'Wales' and 'Welsh' although the native Britons probably hated the term at first. Britons preferred to regard themselves as 'Cymric' or 'Cymru' (pronounced Cimree) and this is what Welsh speakers still prefer today.

Wall to Wall Welsh

Place-names show some evidence for the Welsh Celts who once inhabited northern England. Many Anglo-Saxon place-names originally contained the word 'Walh' and these refer to the native Welsh inhabitants who once lived there. Examples include Walworth near Darlington or Walburn and Walshford in Yorkshire and several places called Walton in Lancashire and Cheshire. Wallasey near Liverpool means 'island of the Welsh' while Wallish Walls near Consett, County Durham means 'Walls of the Welshmen'. By studying the earliest spellings of these aforementioned place-names we know that they refer to Welsh or Britons rather than a wall structure.

The only problem with the word 'Walh' in Anglo-Saxon place-names is that it can also mean 'serf' or 'servant' rather than Welshman or Briton. However most of the Britons were employed or regarded as servants by the Anglo-Saxons, so the distinction is not critical. In the south of England the word 'Walh' also gave rise to the name Cornwall. This is a reminder that the ancient Cornish language was very closely related to Welsh and that the Cornish were a distinct tribe of Welshmen.

So, did most of the Britons pack up their trunks and head for the Welsh Mountains to escape the Anglo-Saxon raids? It seems unlikely. Britons fought to defend their land against the invaders and although the northern Britons were defeated at the Battle of Catterick in 598AD, they did not go down without a fight. Welsh speakers from as far a part as Edinburgh and North Wales fought for the Britons at Catterick.

After defeat, some Britons may have fled west to Wales, which is the traditional view of their fate. However it is likely that many Britons stayed, to be absorbed by the new population, although many would undoubtedly end up as slaves. Whatever their fate, those who survived would have to adopt the language of the Anglo-Saxons.

York - from Yew Tree to Yorvik

The Romans knew York as 'Eboracum' but this name was based on a more ancient Celtic name. It is thought to have derived from 'Eburos', a Celtic personal name meaning Yew tree. When the later Anglo-Saxons arrived they are thought to have misunderstood the name and renamed it 'Eoforwic' meaning 'wild boar settlement'. When the Vikings arrived they changed it again, renaming it 'Jorvik' - pronounced Yorvik. Sometime during the late Viking period the name Yorvik was clipped and it came to be pronounced 'York'. York is sometimes thought to be the longest continuously inhabited settlement in the British Isles.

Do Northerners have Celtic blood?

Studies carried out at University College London for a BBC TV programme about the Vikings in 2001 showed that the people of Britain have a strong Celtic element in their genes. It showed that Wales and Ireland have a particularly high Celtic influence in their genes as we might expect, but the study also showed that there was a large Celtic presence in the population of England.

In fact the study showed that although the Celtic make up of Scotland was also very high, it was not noticeably higher than the south of England. Strangely, in the north of England, the Celtic genetic presence was slightly less than in Scotland or the south, but even here, it was too significant to be ignored.

The study looked at men from various small towns in localities across Britain. It selected small towns largely untouched by industrial growth in recent centuries and studied men whose paternal families had lived in those localities for a number of generations. This ensured that population movements in more recent centuries did not distort the results.

DNA samples were taken from the men to study the Y chromosome, carried only by men and passed from fathers to sons. The chromosomes were compared with those of people in Norway, Denmark, Schleswig-Holstein and parts of the 'Celtic' western Ireland where there is known to have been very little outside influence within the genetic population.

Yeavering Bell, Northumberland. The summit is the site of a Celtic fort, the land at the base was later the site of a palace belonging to the Anglo-Saxon kings of Northumberland.

The study was able to identify people of ancient Norwegian or Celtic descent in Britain, but discovered that Anglo-Saxons and Danes were impossible to tell apart. For the purposes of the study Anglo-Saxons were grouped together with the Danes and it was found that their

collective influence was most noticeable in northern and eastern England and was particularly high in York. This is perhaps not surprising as York was an important Anglo-Saxon town and later the Danish capital of the North.

In Penrith, the only Cumbrian town featured in the study, the influence of the Anglo-Saxons/Danes was found to be noticeably weak compared to other places in the North. Here the genetic study demonstrated a very strong Celtic survival and a significant Norwegian influence. This is interesting because place-names and history indicate that Cumbria was an important area of Celtic survival and high Norwegian settlement.

From these genetic results we might conclude that Britain is a melting pot of ancient cultures and that the Anglo-Saxons did not wipe out the Celts. They merely absorbed them into a mixed population.

It seems likely that many people in the north of England today are descended from the ancient Welsh speaking Celts who inhabited the north in the days after the Roman empire and before the Anglo-Saxon conquest.

Celtic and Roman place-names and people

Almondbury: Anglo-Saxon name for place near Huddersfield. It was the site of a Celtic fort. The Anglo-Saxon words burgh and bury often signify a stronghold.

Brigantes: A Celtic tribe that dominated the north in Roman times. Pronounced Brigantees.

Britons: The name given to the native Celtic people of Britain.

Carlisle: From the Celtic word Caer (a fort) and Luel a shortened form of the Roman name Luguvalium.

Caledonia: The Roman name for highland Scotland and its tribes.

Carvetti: Celtic tribe that inhabited Cumberland in Roman times.

Chester: Anglo-Saxon name for a Roman fort.

Corionototae: Celtic tribe that inhabited the Tyne valley area in Roman times.

Coritani: Celtic tribe that inhabited Lincolnshire in Roman times.

Cornovii: Celtic tribe that inhabited Shropshire and Cheshire in Roman times.

Craven: District of Yorkshire with an ancient Welsh name.

Cumberland: Takes its name from Cymru - the Welsh.

Deceangli: Celtic tribe that inhabited North Wales in Roman times.

Derwent: Celtic river-name meaning 'oak river'.

Dumbarton: Scottish place-name means fortress of the Britons. It was the capital of the Celtic kingdom of Strathclyde.

Eboracum: Roman name for York. Derives from a name meaning Yew Tree.

Elmet: A Welsh kingdom in southern and western Yorkshire.

Gabrantovices: Celtic tribe that inhabited the North Yorkshire coastal area in Roman times.

Gododdin: A ancient Celtic kingdom in southern Scotland.

Hibernia: The Roman name for Ireland.

Humber: From an ancient name Ahmbas meaning 'good-well river'.

Ince: From a Celtic word Inys meaning island.

Law: Anglo-Saxon word for a hill. They were often topped with Celtic hill forts.

Leeds: From Leodis, the name of a Celtic region in Yorkshire.

Linn: Celtic word for a lake.

Lopocares: Celtic tribe that inhabited the Tyne valley area in Roman times.

Lough: Northumbrian and Irish word of Celtic origin meaning lake.

Mamucium: Roman name for Manchester.

Makerfield: District in Lancashire, probably a Celtic kingdom in ancient times.

Morecambe: Celtic place-name in Lancashire meaning 'sea bay'.

Nidd: Yorkshire river with Celtic name meaning 'shining'.

Ouse: Yorkshire river with Celtic name meaning 'water or river'.

Parisi: Celtic tribe that inhabited East Yorkshire in Roman times.

Pen-y-Ghent: Yorkshire hill with a Celtic name.

Rheged: A Celtic kingdom in Cumberland.

Scots: A Celtic tribe originating from Ireland that settled in Caledonia.

Setantii: Celtic tribe inhabiting the Fylde peninsula near Blackpool in Roman times.

Tees: A Celtic river name meaning something like 'boiling river'.

Tectoverdi: Celtic tribe that inhabited the Tyne valley area in Roman times.

Tyne: A Celtic river name meaning 'water'.

Vedra: Roman name for the River Wear.

Votadini: Celtic tribe that inhabited Northumberland and southern Scotland in Roman times.

Welsh/Wales: From 'Waelisc' the Anglo-Saxon name for the Britons.

Wigan: From an ancient Celtic name Tref Wigan. Its meaning is unknown.

Wyre: Lancashire river with Celtic name meaning 'winding'.

Part Three:
Kingdom of the North

The Kingdom of Northumbria

Part Three:
Kingdom of the North

The Kingdom of Northumbria

Today, the north of England is often thought to form a distinct region within the United Kingdom, but in Anglo-Saxon times it was more than just a region, it was a kingdom in its own right. This was the Kingdom of Northumbria and was founded by a people called the Angles in the seventh century. Northumbria encompassed almost all the land covered by the northern counties of today. Cumbria, Lancashire, Yorkshire, Durham and Northumberland were all part of Northumbria as were the areas now covered by the present urban regions of Tyne and Wear, Teesside, Merseyside and Greater Manchester. Only those areas of Merseyside and Greater Manchester to the south of the River Mersey lay outside the Northumbrian kingdom.

The Mersey was the south western boundary of Northumbria, so Liverpool and Manchester lay on the southern fringes of the Northumbrian kingdom. The southern boundaries of Northumbria were almost identical to the traditional southern boundaries of Lancashire and Yorkshire. For example Sheffield, which lies on the southern edge of Yorkshire, also lay on the southern edge of the Kingdom of Northumbria. Indeed traces of earthworks marking the southern boundary of the Northumbrian kingdom can be found in the southern outskirts of the present day cities of Manchester and Sheffield.

In the east, the Humber marked the southern boundary of Northumbria - hence the name 'North Humbria' which literally means 'north of the Humber'. However, the Angles who founded the kingdom originally called themselves the Humbresnes and lived on both sides of the Humber in Lincolnshire and Yorkshire.

For most of its Anglo-Saxon history, Lincolnshire on the south side of the Humber was known as Lindsey and belonged to the kingdom of Mercia. Lindsey was regarded as disputed territory and fell under Northumbrian control for a period of time.

The counties of Cheshire, Staffordshire, Nottinghamshire and Derbyshire were all situated in Mercia as were other midland counties like Warwickshire, Leicestershire and Northamptonshire. In modern times the County of Cheshire is often regarded as part of the north because of its close connections with the urban regions of Manchester and Liverpool, but in Anglo-Saxon times it was undoubtedly part of the midlands. The cathedral in the city of Chester was built to house the remains of St Werburgh who was a member of the Mercian royal family.

England the 'Angle Land'

Compared to the Celts, the Saxons and Angles who founded kingdoms like Northumbria have left a much greater legacy in the dialect and place-names of England. Arriving in Britain from around 450 AD, many of the earliest Anglo-Saxons were employed as mercenaries by the native Britons. The Anglo-Saxons soon saw the opportunity for the conquest of Britain and they began the full-scale invasion of our shores. The Anglo-Saxons were comprised of two major groups of people called the 'Angles' and the 'Saxons', but it was the Angles who really settled in the north of England. The Angles came from southern Jutland, near to where the boundaries of Germany and Denmark meet today. Today this region is called Schleswig-Holstein and it is here that we can still find a small district called Angeln. The name is a remarkable reminder of the Angles' original homeland.

It was the Angles who founded the Kingdoms of Northumbria and Mercia as well as the kingdom of East Anglia. East Anglia takes its name from being the 'kingdom of the eastern Angles'. Most importantly of all, the Angles gave their name to 'England' - which literally means 'Angle Land'. England was really a land of both Angles and Saxons, but the two people were so closely related that they are often just known as Anglo-Saxons or English. However it was the Angles who really established the very concept of Northern England - the 'Northern Angle Land', although northern England was known as 'Northumbria'.

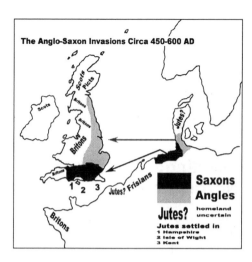

The Anglo-Saxon Invasions Circa 450-600 AD.

The English of Old

Angles and Saxons spoke very closely related Germanic languages and could easily understand each other. However, being Germanic is not the same as being German.

> **Who were the Anglo-Saxons?**
>
> The Saxons were a Germanic people, first mentioned in the second century BC when they were known to have inhabited southern Jutland and the area around the River Elbe. They gradually expanded westward along the German coast. The Angles lived just to the north of the Saxons and from around 450 AD both groups of people began their invasion and settlement of Britain. The Angles and Saxons worshipped pagan gods, chief amongst whom was Woden, known as Odin by the later Vikings. Wednesday takes its name from the god Woden.

The language of modern Germany is just one of several languages, old and new, that can be described as 'Germanic'. Germanic languages of today include Dutch, Flemish, English and the Scandinavian languages of

Swedish, Norwegian, Icelandic and Danish.

students know all of these dialects as 'Old English' or 'O.E' for short.

Who were the Germans?

Although we think of Germans as people from Germany, the term Germanic can actually be applied to a much larger group of people stretching over a wide area of Europe. For example, the Scandinavian people of Iceland, Norway, Denmark and Sweden (but not Finland) are Germanic. The Dutch and the Flemish people of Belgium and the Netherlands are also Germanic, as were the ancient Franks who gave their name to France and the Anglo-Saxons who gave their name to England. Even the ancient Lombards of northern Italy were Germanic.

The earliest Germanic people lived in northern Germany, Denmark and southern Sweden. From here they spread northwards into Scandinavia and south into Europe. Here they gradually replaced the Celtic culture that dominated central Europe. By the first century BC the Germans had divided up into several distinct peoples who came into increasing contact with the Romans. Most Germanic people were not conquered by the Romans and lay outside the Roman Empire.

Many Germanic people were noted for their tall fair-haired appearance and were regarded by the Romans as barbaric, troublesome warriors. Germanic tribes or people found at various stages of early European history included the Vandals, Teutons, Cimbri, Goths, Burgundians, Lombards, Alemanni, Saxons and Angles. Many of the Germanic people were a threat to the Roman army, although the Germanic people of northern Scandinavia known as the Vikings did not rise to prominence until a much later period.

The Jutes

Most of our information about the Anglo-Saxon invasion of Britain comes from archaeology or from the writings of the Venerable Bede. Bede was the first Anglo-Saxon historian, who lived at Jarrow on the River Tyne. He mentioned that the Jutes settled in Kent, the Isle of Wight and part of southern Hampshire. It is usually thought that the Jutes came from Jutland, but archaeological evidence suggests that they actually came from the area around the mouth of the Rhine, although this area was normally associated with the Franks.

When linguistic experts talk about 'Old English' they aren't just talking about any past form of English. Old English is specifically the language of the Angles and Saxons. In other words it was the language of the English as spoken before the Norman Conquest of 1066. Of course there was also significant Viking influence in the language after 900 AD.

Sexy Southerners

The Saxons came from the area along the northern German coast. Their homeland stretched from the southern reaches of Denmark towards Frisia and Holland. When they arrived in Britain, they settled mainly in the south of England, where the southern, eastern, western and middle Saxons established the kingdoms of Sussex, Essex, Wessex and Middlesex. The word 'sex' in these names comes from 'Seax', a kind of weapon from which the Saxons took their name.

In England the Anglo-Saxons probably arrived in tribal groups that were already well established on the continent. When they settled in England various tribal dialects would develop into regional dialects like Mercian or Northumbrian. Language

One expert has estimated that about eighty per cent of the words in a carefully researched 'Dialect Dictionary' of Northumbrian or North-Eastern English words would be O.E or Anglo-Saxon in origin. This figure has been disputed and it now seems that there is also a strong influence from Old Norse and other elements. This means that the Northumbrian dialect of today is not quite as pure Anglo-Saxon as is often claimed. However it seems the Northumbrian dialect does seem far more Anglo-Saxon than English itself.

English and Scottish are Germanic

If we were to travel back in time to the Anglo-Saxon age, we would find that the Anglo-Saxon language was more like a foreign language than the later English spoken at the time of Chaucer or Shakespeare. Nevertheless the most basic words in the English language are often Anglo-Saxon in origin. They include 'on', 'in', 'it', 'at' 'but', 'man', 'child', 'brother', 'sister', 'eat', 'drink', 'fight' and 'love'. Strangely, despite this important list of basic words you can still only find a small percentage of words in an English dictionary that are actually Anglo-Saxon or 'O.E.' in origin. Most words come from other sources like Scandinavian, French, Latin and even Greek.

However, there are many Anglo-Saxon words that are no longer used in standard English, that have managed to survive in local dialects. For example, many of the dialect words used in North-East England are of Anglo-Saxon origin as are many Scottish words.

Burns Country

In Scotland a 'Burn' is a stream but Burn is actually an Anglo-Saxon word that was once used throughout England. Northumberland and north Durham are now the only parts of England to call streams burns.

The Haliwerfolk

The people of County Durham were known in ancient times as the Haliwerfolk. Pronounced 'Haley wer folk' this means the 'Holy man people' and refers to their guardianship of Saint Cuthbert's remains. The word 'wer' meaning 'man' is Anglo-Saxon and is also used in the word werewolf, meaning 'man wolf'.

Anglo-Saxon 'Toons'

If place-names are a reliable indication of where the people of the north originated, then Anglo-Saxons must have had a major influence. Most of the place-names in England and lowland Scotland are Anglo-Saxon in origin and these far outweigh place-names of any other origin.

Most obvious are place-names that end in 'ton'. This was originally pronounced 'toon' in the Anglo-Saxon language. Ton occurs in thousands of British place-names.

The word 'ton' in Anglo-Saxon meant enclosure, settlement, farm or estate, it did not mean town, although the word town developed from the word 'ton'. Nevertheless, we can see that the Geordie and Scots word 'toon' meaning town is close to the old pronunciation of ton and may have a very old origin. The other well-known Anglo-Saxon place-name suffix is 'ham' meaning 'homestead', 'village' or 'estate'. It occurs in places like Billingham and was originally pronounced 'hame'.

'Ton' and 'ham' are often preceded in place-names by the word 'ing' as in Darlington, Warrington, Cottingham and Billingham in the North of England or as in Haddington near Edinburgh. 'Ing' usually describes a family or tribal group of Anglo-Saxons. For example Haddington near Edinburgh is thought to have belonged to a small family group headed by an Anglo-Saxon called Haden.

Similarities of Scottish and Northumbrian

We have already said that the Northumbrian or North East dialect has a strong Anglo-Saxon influence. The same is also true of the kind of English spoken in Scotland. This is because the Angles colonised a large part of what is now lowland Scotland. The Angle Kingdom of Northumbria stretched as far north as the Firth of Forth.

Sassenachs are Saxons

Scots and Irish made no distinction between the Angles and the Saxons. As far as they were concerned, all English people were and still are 'Sassenachs' - even though this is actually the Gaelic word for a 'Saxon'.

In the land between the Tweed and the Forth, which is now part of Scotland, the Angles had seized the territory from the native Welsh speakers during the formative years of the Kingdom of Northumbria. Place-name evidence demonstrates that the Angles extensively settled there. In fact Anglo-Saxon place-names can be found along most of the eastern coast of Scotland. This may also reflect English linguistic influence that occurred there in later centuries.

Anglo-Saxon Words

Angles were Scandinavian
Angle speech was closer to Scandinavian than that of the Saxons. It was the Angles who settled in the North of England. So there was Scandinavian influence in northern speech and culture even before the Vikings came to England.

The Number Fower
Some North Easterners say 'Fower' for the Number Four. The Anglo-Saxons said 'Feower'. The Frisians still say 'Fjouwer'.

Gannin' Oot
In the Dutch and Flemish language 'Ut Gang' (pronounced Oot-Gan) means 'Exit'. In Geordie 'to exit is to 'Gan Oot'. The Anglo-Saxons also understood Gan and Oot.

Clathes
Anglo-Saxons called Clothes 'Clathas' and this is probably the origin of the Northern word 'Claes'.

Since lowland Scotland was once part of Northumbria, the language of the Angles was spoken in the land between the Tweed and the Forth. For this reason, the speech of lowland Scotland has retained many features in common with northern England. So in studying northern dialects its is important to remember that lowland Scotland, including Edinburgh, was once part of Northumbria and that the people of these areas once spoke Northumbrian.

When Scotland became a nation in its own right, Edinburgh became its capital and the Angle dialect spoken in and around the city became the Scottish nation's official language, eventually replacing the Gaelic spoken in the Highland region. In time, the Northumbrian spoken in lowland Scotland developed many distinct features of its own. In Medieval times the form of English spoken in Scotland was known as 'Inglis'. Today it is known as 'Scots'.

Longest Place-Name

Blakehopeburnhaugh in Redesdale, Northumberland claims to be England's, longest place-name with 18 letters. The name is Anglo-Saxon and means 'Black Valley Stream with flat meadowland. However it has a rival less than a mile away called Cottonshopeburnfoot. The Ordnance Survey record Cottonshopeburnfoot as two words - Cottonshopeburn Foot.

Like the Northumbrian dialect, Scots is actually closer to Anglo-Saxon than the English spoken in England. The Scots language has many similarities to the dialects of Northern England, because both developed from the ancient Northumbrian language. This is why

Anglo-Saxon words like 'gan' and 'lang' are as familiar to Scots as they are to Geordies, Northumbrians, Yorkshiremen or Cumbrians. The irony is that Northumbrian is now usually described as a 'dialect' while Scots is usually accepted as a 'language'.

Bernicians and Deirans

The Angles called their kingdom in northern England, 'Northumbria', but Northumbria was originally two separate kingdoms called Bernicia and Deira. We don't know the meaning of the names Bernicia and Deira, but they may have developed from earlier Celtic kingdoms.

Deira was originally the region just north of the River Humber in East Yorkshire and developed from the tribal region of the 'Humbresnes'. Deira corresponds very closely to the territory occupied by the Celtic Parisi tribe of Roman times. It is very possible that the Angles took over a Celtic kingdom called Deira, and that this Celtic kingdom had developed from the Parisian tribal area, but we do not know for sure. The Angles claimed that it was an Angle chieftain called Aelle or Ella who founded Deira.

An Anglian chief also established the Kingdom of Bernicia. His name was Ida the Flamebearer and he seized the Celtic fortress of Din Guayroi from the native Celtic Britons in 547 AD. We know this fortress today as Bamburgh. Bernicia may have developed from land settled by the Angles in this area or

from Anglian settlements further south along the River Tyne.

Bamburgh Castle stands on the site of the ancient capital of Bernicia.

Bernicia expanded under Ida's grandson who was called Ethelfrith. He extended the kingdom's boundaries as far south as the River Tees and as far to the west as the Lake District. Deira, the kingdom to the south of the Tees also expanded until it encompassed all of Yorkshire and Lancashire with York as its capital. The Mersey and the Humber formed Deira's southern boundary. To the south of this boundary lay another expanding Angle kingdom called Mercia - the kingdom of the Midlands. The names of Mersey and Mercia both come from an Anglo-Saxon word meaning 'boundary or border'.

Bernicia got the upper hand over Deira when Ethelfrith seized the rival kingdom. He thus unified the two to form the Kingdom of Northumbria. Ethelfrith remained king until he was defeated and killed by Edwin of Deira in a great battle at Hatfield near Doncaster. Edwin succeeded Ethelfrith as king.

The next great king of Northumbria was a Bernician called Oswald, but in the centuries to come power passed back and forth between Bernicia and Deira. Rivalry between the two regions was a major feature of Northumbria's history and would weaken the kingdom at the time of the Viking raids.

Celtic Northumbria

The Kingdom of Northumbria established by the Angles would reach moments of greatness. During the reigns of Edwin, Oswald and Oswy it was the most powerful kingdom in Britain. With the introduction of Christianity, the Northumbrian kingdom became a great centre for arts and learning and its influence was felt all over Europe. By this time most people in Northern England spoke a form of the Anglo-Saxon language known as Northumbrian, although Celtic may have been spoken in some remoter areas of the North.

On the whole the Anglo-Saxon language and culture now dominated, but there were other cultural influences. We know for example that some of the earliest Christian monasteries in the North were established through strong Irish influence. Aidan, the first Bishop of Lindisfarne was an Irishman while Aldfrid one of the most important Northumbrian kings also had strong Irish connections.

We can also see a strong Irish connection in terms of art. There are great similarities between the Book of Kells in Ireland and the Lindisfarne Gospels in Northumbria, which both date from the Anglo-Saxon period. Celtic missionaries and monks settled in the Northumbrian Kingdom from Ireland and even an Irish princess called Hieu is known to have established a monastery in the North at Hartlepool. Whether the Irish of this period left any trace in our population is difficult to tell, although the peculiar Celtic lilt of Lindisfarne's island dialect may have ancient roots that go back to these times.

After the Synod of Whitby in 664 AD, Celtic Christianity was abandoned in Northumbria in favour of a kind of Christianity that had developed in Rome. After this period, York, rather than Lindisfarne, became the focus for Christianity in Northumbria.

Bede - The Scholar of Jarrow

The most famous Anglo-Saxon scholar of all times was the Venerable Bede of Jarrow. Bede was an Angle and spoke an old form of Northumbrian. He was born in Sunderland and lived most of his life at Jarrow on the Tyne. Bede would understand some aspects of the Northern English dialect of today, perhaps better than he would understand modern English.

The Jarrow Tribe

The place-name Jarrow comes from an Anglo-Saxon tribe called the 'Gyrwe'. This was also the name of a tribe that lived near the Wash in East Anglia. The name means 'marsh dwellers'. Ripon is another Anglo-Saxon name with tribal origins. These types of names are quite rare.

A translation of an Anglo-Saxon song written in Northumbria at the time, about Bede's Death describes the soul leaving the body. It clearly demonstrates how the old language translates into North-East dialect better than it would into English.

The translation of Bede's Death Song was undertaken by the nineteenth century Northumbrian dialect expert Richard Oliver Heslop who demonstrated how rhythmically the Anglo-Saxon song flows in the local dialect:

Afore thor need-fare
Yen is nivvor mair
Wise in thowt,
Than he owt
Think what he can
On his way gan
What tiv his ghaist
O' good or ill maist
After deeth day
Doom then may say.

Common Anglo-Saxon place-name elements

Ac: - Oak.
Billing: - hill.
Black: - from Anglo-Saxon Blaec meaning Black.
Bottle: - 'abode' from Anglo-Saxon bothl.
Broom: - gorse.
Burgh/Bury/Borough/Brough: - from the Anglo-Saxon word 'Burh' meaning fortified place or manor.
Burn/Bourn: - from the Anglo-Saxon 'Burna' meaning stream
Chester/Caster: - from 'Ceaster', the Anglo-Saxon name for the site of a Roman fort.
Clif/Cliffe: - a hill or embankment, not necessarily a steep cliff as today.
Clough: - from the Anglo-Saxon 'Cluh', a ravine.
Dene/Dean/Den: - a small wooded valley.
Dun/Don: - a hill.
Field: - means open countryside. From the Anglo-Saxon Feld. Does not mean enclosed piece of land as it does in today's English language.
Ford/Forth: - A river crossing.
Ham: - a homestead.
Haugh: - from 'halh', meaning flat land near a river.
Heugh: - from 'hoh' a hill spur.
Hope: - from 'hop' a side valley.
Ing: - Tribal or kinship group.
Ley/Lea: - from the Anglo-Saxon leah meaning clearing in a wood or meadowland.
Law/Low: A hill.
Shaw: - A wood.
Stock: - means log or religious settlement.
Thorn: - a thorn tree.
Ton: - from tun, an enclosure, farm or estate.
Wick: - a trading place.
Worth: - an enclosed settlement.

Anglo-Saxon Place-names in the North East

Acomb: Near Hexham but also near York. From the Anglo Saxon Akum meaning 'oaks'.

Alnwick: Means farm on the River Aln. Aln is a Celtic river-name.

Ashington: From Aesec Dene the Ash Tree Valley.

Bamburgh: Bebba's Burgh, named after the wife of Ethelfrith, the King of Northumbria.

Berwick: 'Barley farm'.

Billingham: Ham means homestead. Billinge was a kind of small hill.

Blaydon: 'Blaec Don' - the black hill.

Brandon: Broom Don - the gorse hill.

Darlington: The farm of Deornoth's people.

Elswick: Elfsige's Farm.

Ferryhill: From Fiergen hill. Fiergen means wooded hill.

Gateshead: Means Goat's Head, perhaps from some kind of totem or crest.

Gosforth: The goose ford.

Hartlepool: Place-name derives from the Anglo-Saxon 'Heruteu' meaning the 'island of the stag'.

Hebburn: Tyneside place-name, from High Byrgen meaning high tumulus.

Hetton: From Heop Dun. Rose hope hill.

Jarrow: A tribal name meaning the marsh or fen dwellers.

Lanchester: Probably the 'long Roman fort'.

Langbaurgh: In Cleveland. Means the long hill.

Langley: The long clearing.

Lindisfarne: Perhaps 'The place of the travellers from Lindsey or Lincolnshire'.

Middlesbrough: The Middle stronghold or manor.

Morpeth: Moor path or hill.

Norton: Teesside. Means the northern farm.

Prudhoe: In the Tyne Valley. Means Pruda's Hoh or hill spur.

Seaham: Seaside homestead.

Sedgefield: Open land belonging to Cedd.

Shildon: The 'shelf hill'.

Spennymoor: The hedged moorland.

Stanhope: Stony valley.

Stanley: Stony clearing.

Sunderland: Sundered Land, land kept aside for a special purpose.

Whickham: Homestead with a quick set hedge.

Witton: Wood Farm.

Wolsingham: Weardale, Durham. Means Wulfsige's people's homestead.

Yarm: Town on the River Tees. Derives from the Anglo-Saxon Gearum meaning fish weirs.

Anglo-Saxon Place-names in Cumbria and the North West

Accrington: From Accerntun meaning the 'farm where acorns grew'.

Allerton: Near Liverpool. Means 'Alder Tree Farm'.

Alston: Aldhun's Farm.

Ashton in Makerfield: Ash Tree settlement located in old Celtic region of Makerfield.

Ashton under Lyne: Ash Tree settlement in the 'Lyne' an old Celtic name meaning 'elm tree forest'.

Atherton: Near Manchester means Aethelhere's farm.

Bacup: From Baec, a ridge and hop - a valley.

Barnoldswick: Beornwulf's Farm.

Blackburn: Means the black stream. There is a stream here called the Blackwater.

Blackpool: The dark coloured pool.

Bolton: From 'bothal ton' meaning building-farm.

Bootle: Derives from Bothal meaning abode or dwelling.

Burnley: From 'Brun Ley' meaning the Brown coloured clearing.

Bury: From 'burgh' meaning stronghold or manor.

Carnforth: Means ford with cranes - a kind of bird. It has the same meaning as Cornforth in Durham.

Chester: Named from the site of a Roman fort.

Chorley: The clearing of the churl/peasant.

Chorlton: Farm of the churl/peasant.

Cleveleys: Near Blackpool. Means hill clearings.

Everton: In Liverpool, from Efor ton - the wild boar farm.

Fylde: District in Blackpool area. From gefilde meaning 'a plain', peninsula.

Haweswater: Hafr's Water.

Heysham: From Haes-Ham the brushwood homestead.

Huyton: Near Liverpool. From 'hythe ton' meaning landing place farm.

Hyde: Near Stockport. Means a hide or measured unit of land.

Knowsley: The clearing or 'ley' belonging to Cynewulf.

Manchester: Mamcester - fort of the breast like hill.

Oswaldwhistle: A tongue of land formed by a fork or 'twisla' that belonged to Oswald.

Prescot: The priest's cottage.

Preston: The priest's farm.

Prestwich: Near Manchester means the priest's farm.

Ramsbottom: Means the bottom or valley where ramsons or wild garlic grew.

Rawtenstall: From 'rough tun-stall' meaning rough farm site.

Ribchester: Site of Roman fort on River Ribble.

Rishton: Near Blackburn Means the farm where rushes grew.

Runcorn: From Rum and Cofa meaning roomy bay/cove. It is located on the Mersey estuary.

Sale: From 'salh' meaning Willow tree.

Salford: The ford where Willow trees grew.

Thirlmere: Means the lake with an opening.

Ulverston: Wulfhere's farm.

Warrington: From 'Waering ton' meaning farm near the river with a weir. It is located on the Mersey.

Workington: Means Weorc's people's homestead.

Anglo-Saxon Place-names in Yorkshire

Aldbrough/Aldborough: Means the 'old fort'.

Ampleforth: Ford where 'ampre' (sorrel) grew.

Barnsley: The Clearing belonging to Beorn.

Barton: Barley farm.

Batley: Clearing belonging to Bata.

Bedale: 'Bedas Halh' - a secret corner belonging to someone called Bede.

Bingley: Clearing belonging to Bynna.

Bradford: The Broad Ford.

Bridlington: Beorktel's people's farm.

Brompton: Broom Ton the gorsey farm.

Cottingham: Farm belonging to Cota and his people.

Dewsbury: Dewi's burgh or stronghold.

Doncaster: 'Site of a Roman fort on the River Don'.

Dore: Near Sheffield, the door or pass between Mercia and Northumbria.

Filey: From Fif-ley - the five clearings.

Garforth: Gaera's Ford

Goodmanham: Homestead of Godmund and his people. It was the site of a pagan shrine.

Harrogate: From 'Har-low-Gata' meaning Grey-Hill-Road.

Haworth: From Haga's (Haya's) Worth. Meaning hedge enclosure.

Headingley: The clearing of Hedde's people.

Heckmondwike: Farm belonging to Heahmond.

Huddersfield: Huddraed's open land.

Ilkley: Ley means clearing. Derives from a Roman name Olicana.

Keighley: Cyhha's clearing.

Knaresborough: Knar, a stump plus borough or burgh - a fortified place.

Masham: Maesa's Homestead.

Northallerton: Northern Allerton - Aelfhere's farm.

Otley: Ota's clearing.

Pickering: An Anglo-Saxon tribal name meaning people of the pointed hill.

Pocklington: Pocel's peoples' farm.

Pudsey: Means Pudoc's island.

Ripon: North Yorkshire. Thought to take its name from an Anglo-Saxon tribe called Hyrpe.

Sheffield: 'Open land near the River Sheaf'. Sheaf means 'boundary'.

Shipley: Sheep clearing.

Shipton: Sheep Farm.

Tadcaster: Site of Roman fort belonging to an Anglo-Saxon called Tada.

Todmorden: Means Tota's boundary (Maere) valley (Dene).

Wakefield: Field belonging to Wacca.

Wensley: Originally Wodensley the clearing dedicated to the pagan god Woden. Wensley gives its name to Wensleydale.

Part Four:
The Vikings and Yorkshire

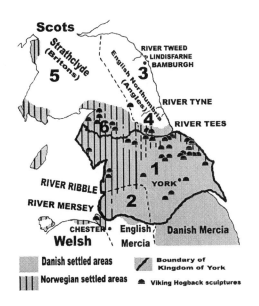

The Viking North, Circa 800-1000 AD

1. *Viking Northumbria; 2. Between Ribble and Mersey;*
3. *Bernicia; 4. St. Cuthbert's Land; 5. Strathclyde; 6. Cumberland.*

Part Four :
The Vikings and Yorkshire

The Viking North

In 793 AD a raiding party of Vikings attacked the Northumbrian monastery of Lindisfarne in an unprecedented attack. Raids continued throughout the following century until eventually in 866 AD the Danes embarked on a major invasion of Northern England. They ultimately seized the Northumbrian capital of Eoforwik which they renamed Jorvik. We know this city today as York.

Viking Britain. Black areas show Norwegian settlement, grey represents the Danish settled areas.

York was the capital of the southern part of Northumbria, a region known as Deira. Deira was comprised of Yorkshire and Lancashire and was captured and extensively settled by the Danes after 866. By comparison, most of Bernicia, the region to the north of the Tees, appears to have seen very little Danish settlement although it is not clear why.

Viking words in the English Language

If you look in an English dictionary you can find many words that are described as 'O.N'. These are English words of Viking, origin as O.N means 'Old Norse'. Viking words in the English language include 'skull', 'leg', 'freckle', 'meek', 'rotten', 'clasp', 'crawl', 'dazzle', 'take', 'scream', 'lift', 'trust' and 'husband'. The Vikings also introduced 'they', 'them' and 'their' to the English language.

The Anglo-Saxons did not use any of these words until the Vikings arrived. So the language of the Vikings changed the vocabulary of the English language forever. However, it did not replace the Anglo-Saxon speech altogether. Anglo-Saxon and Viking speech were very closely related and this enabled the two languages to merge together naturally over time.

Sometimes the differences between the two languages were so subtle that they could produce interesting variations. For example, one feature of the Viking language was that the 'Sh' sound of Anglo-Saxon speech often became 'Sk' in Viking. The Anglo-Saxon word 'shirt' originally meant 'garment', and had the same meaning as the Viking word 'skirt'. Today these two words refer to two different kinds of garment. Another example of the sh/sk phenomenon is the place-name Marske-by-the-Sea on the Yorkshire - Cleveland coast. The pronunciation of this name was affected by Viking speech. It means 'marsh by the sea'. Old Norse has also had a profound influence on the English language at a regional level and has influenced dialects like Cumbrian and Yorkshire.

Who were the Vikings?

The Vikings were Scandinavian warriors from Denmark, Norway and Sweden. They were typically a tall, blonde or fair-haired race of Germanic people who evolved in Scandinavia over a number of centuries. They had developed from smaller scattered groups of people employed in farming, fishing and hunting. Over time the Scandinavian population expanded and developed into larger tribal groups who would ultimately become the Norwegians, Danes and Swedes.

For most Scandinavians life was closely tied to the sea. This is not surprising if we consider the geographical nature of the Scandinavian nations. Denmark, a relatively flat country with much arable land is comprised of a mainland peninsula that juts into the sea alongside several neighbouring islands. Norway is dominated by a mountainous landscape where numerous sea inlets called 'fjords' provide the only suitable habitation.

In such a maritime landscape ships became a principal means of trade and travel and the Vikings became the best shipbuilders in the world. As population increased and land was increasingly divided in Scandinavia, the desire to seek land and treasure further afield increased. The sophisticated Viking ships enabled the Vikings go in search of booty far from their homelands.

The monasteries on the eastern coasts of England, Scotland and Ireland provided wealthy, yet vulnerable, undefended targets and were amongst the earliest destinations of the Viking raiders. Norwegians and Danes increasingly began to raid and settle Britain, although some Vikings explored lands much further to the north and west. Norwegians founded colonies in Iceland, Greenland and even, for a short time, in North America.

In the British Isles, the Danes settled mainly in northern and eastern England. Norwegians by contrast preferred the western areas, settling in Ireland, the northern coasts of Scotland, the Orkneys, Shetlands, Western Isles and the Isle of Man. Norwegians also settled on the coasts of Wales, Cumbria and certain coastal areas of Lancashire and Cheshire. The Swedes had little part in the settlement of Britain. The Swedes concentrated their raiding efforts in the east of Europe. One tribe of Swedes called the 'Rus' who settled in Kiev played a major part in the settlement and naming of Russia, although Russia was largely a Slavic nation.

It is possible that the Vikings considered Bernicia to have poorer quality agricultural land and its capture may have simply over-stretched Viking military resources. The Danes preferred to settle in the fertile regions of Yorkshire as well as in East Anglia and the East Midlands. In the East Midlands or 'East Mercia' the Danes established many settlements in what are now the counties of Nottinghamshire, Derbyshire, Lincolnshire and Leicestershire.

There was little or no Danish settlement in the western midlands or in southern England. Thus it can be seen that the areas of Danish settlement in England were clearly defined. A boundary line was drawn from the mouth of the Thames to the River Dee at Chester in the North West of England. This boundary separated the 'Danelaw' in the north from the lands of the Saxon king, Alfred the Great, in the south. Lands north of this boundary were subjected to Danish laws and customs, those to the south remained Anglo-Saxon.

This does not mean that the Anglo-Saxons and Celts were wiped out in the Viking settled areas. There would be considerable intermixing of people, so that the people of the Danelaw were probably best described as Anglo-Danes. Of course the people of Viking descent were most likely to hold the positions of power, since they had been the victorious conquerors.

Viking Europe, 800-1000 AD.

The Yorkshire Danes

The most important area of Danish Viking settlement in the North of England was Yorkshire. This formed the heartland of the Danish Kingdom of Jorvik and was centred upon York. The Danes divided Yorkshire into three parts called 'Ridings' for administrative purposes and these three regions of Yorkshire were to survive for many centuries.

Yorkshire is often referred to by historians as 'Danish Northumbria' and this is effectively what it became after 866 AD. On November 1st 866 AD, the Danes under the leadership of the brothers Ivar the Boneless, Halfdene and Hubba sacked York. At this time Northumbria was suffering from a dynastic struggle between Aelle, the leader of Deira and Osbert the leader of Bernicia. The two men united to defend the great Northumbrian city of York from the Vikings but Osbert was killed during the battle. Aelle suffered from an even more horrendous fate. On March 23, 867 AD, the Vikings subjected him to the horrific Blood Eagle ordeal. His ribs were torn out and folded back to form the shape of an eagle's wings. It was a gruesome way to die, but the Vikings claimed that Aelle had been responsible for the murder of one of their kin.

Many Danes would come to settle at York. Throughout Yorkshire they would establish hundreds of settlements across the region in the decades to come. If place-names are a reliable indication of

Danish settlement, then the lowland areas of the East Riding and North Riding of York saw particularly high levels of Danish settlement. This was particularly the case in the Vale of York.

Grimston hybrids

Many place-names in the Viking settled areas of England show a mixture of both Viking and Anglo-Saxon influence. They often take the form of what are known as Grimston hybrids. This is because the place-name Grimston is a classic example of one such hybrid. It incorporates a Viking personal name Grimm with the Anglo-Saxon place-name element 'ton'. It is sometimes thought that place-names of this type were Anglo-Saxon settlements taken over by Vikings. There are around 50 Grimston hybrid place-names in Yorkshire.

Danish place-names in Yorkshire are often indicated by names ending in 'by' A 'By' was a farm or village of Viking origin and many places in Denmark still end in the letters 'by'. In the lowland vale to the north of York we find many examples of these names including Haxby, Huby, Helperby, Thormanby, Ainderby, Thirkleby, Baldersby, Ferrensby, Kexby, Melmerby, Sowerby, Thirby, Gatenby, Sinderby, Wetherby, Kirby, Kirkby, Cowesby, Boltby, Skewsby and Whenby.

A Viking "Hogback" sculpture from Brompton near Northallerton in North Yorkshire. It appears to depict two bears grasping a tomb.

Yorkshire has over 200 place-names ending in 'by'. Many of these names incorporate the name of a particular Viking settler, although some incorporate other features. For example places called Kirby and Kirkby signify the site of important churches. This is an important point since the Pagan Vikings in Britain would convert to Christianity during the later Viking period. Thorpe is also a common element in Yorkshire place-names. It signifies a smaller outlying farm or hamlet. There are over 150 'thorpe' place-names in Yorkshire.

Hogbacks

Distinctive Viking sculptures called hogbacks are often found in the north. They are possibly grave covers and have a distinctive curved shape with engravings that show Northumbrian as well as Viking influence. Hogbacks have been found at a number of places in the North of England including Sockburn and Gainford on the River Tees on the southern edge of County Durham. Hogbacks have also been found at Penrith in Cumbria, Heysham near Morecambe in Lancashire, at Brompton near Northallerton in North Yorkshire and at Burnsall near Skipton, also in North Yorkshire. There is a great deal of debate as to whether the carvings on these stones depict pagan themes, Christian themes or a fusion of both.

Some Norwegians were Irish

We tend to think of the Vikings who invaded Britain as being either Danes or Norwegians. It comes as a great surprise to learn that many of the Norwegians who invaded Britain actually came from Ireland. In fact many of the Norwegians who settled in northern England were of mixed Irish-Norwegian origin and are known to historians as the Hiberno-

Norse. These Norwegian Irish didn't start to settle in northern England until about forty years after the Danes.

In the early 800s many Norwegians had sailed from Norway to the northern tip of Scotland where they colonised the Orkney and Shetland Islands. In 841 AD Norwegians journeyed further around the western coast of Scotland and eventually settled in Ireland. Here they established a great stronghold at Dublin. It was the most important of a number of Viking towns established along the Irish coast.

Ten years later, in 851 Dublin was seized by the Danes for a short period and it is likely that many Danes settled there, but it remained an important Norwegian colony for over seventy years. The Viking power in Ireland suffered a major setback in 918 AD when the native Irish led by the King of Leinster expelled the now mixed race of Irish-Norwegians from Dublin.

The native Irish had good reason to hate the Norsemen, since the Vikings saw Ireland mainly as a source for their slave-trading activities. Thousands of Irish were captured and enslaved by the Vikings and shipped abroad to North Africa, Spain and places further east. In Ireland, the Norwegians only settled on the coast. When they did venture into the Irish interior, it was for the sole purpose of raiding and capturing slaves.

Norwegians and Danes in Yorkshire

According to a the study of place-names carried out by the place-name expert A.H. Smith in the North Riding of Yorkshire, there is evidence that some Norwegians settled in Yorkshire directly from Norway across the North Sea. This was particularly the case along the Yorkshire and Cleveland coast, south of the River Tees, where names of Norwegian origin are numerous.

Norwegian place-names are also very numerous in the western part of Yorkshire in the Yorkshire Dales. Norwegian place-names in this area are often similar to those found in Cumbria just over the Pennines to the west. Typical Yorkshire Dales place-names like Yockenthwaite, Hebblethwaite, Thackthwaite and Hunderthwaite point to Norwegian origin and would not look at all out of place in Cumbria.

> **The Viking Islands**
>
> Genetic studies and place-names show the highest proportion of people of Norwegian descent in Britain live in the Orkney and Shetland Islands. Many people on Orkney and Shetland continued to speak a Scandinavian language called 'Norn' right up until the seventeenth and eighteenth century.

The place-names of the Yorkshire Dales suggest that there was a strong link between the Vikings of Cumbria and those of the Dales. It is also known that there are very close similarities between the Cumbrian dialect and the dialect of the Yorkshire Dales. Both dialect areas are strongly influenced by the speech of the Vikings. It seems possible that the Norwegian settlers in the Yorkshire Dales came via Cumbria. Perhaps the Norwegians settled in Cumbria at the same time as they were settling in Ireland.

So Norwegians could be found in the eastern part of Yorkshire along the steeply inclined coast of the North York Moors and could also be found in the western part of Yorkshire in the upland Yorkshire Dales. Sandwiched in between the central lowland area of the Vale of York was settled mainly by the Danes. All of this suggests that the Vikings chose their settlements on a 'home from home' basis. Remember that Denmark is a low-lying country, while uplands and mountainous terrain are more typical of Norway.

Irish Corner?

Melsonby, near Scotch Corner is a Viking place-name that incorporates an Irish personal name. It belonged to an 'Irish Viking' called Maelsuithain.

The Vikings of York

In Viking times most of Northern England was a rural landscape, with human settlement concentrated in small farms and villages. The only major urban centre in the north was at York or 'Jorvik', as it was known to the Vikings. York had been the most important Roman settlement in the North and was the most important Angle settlement in the Kingdom of Northumbria. Its importance continued into Viking times when it became the primary Viking settlement in the British Isles. Much of York's Viking past is remembered in the city's Jorvik Museum, but many of the street names in the city also recall the city's Viking heritage.

Sweet Kets

The Viking word 'ket' is sometimes used in the dialects of County Durham and the North East to mean 'a sweet'. The word originally meant meat or flesh of a poor quality. It later came to mean something that was nasty. Parents may have reprimanded their children for eating sweets and described them as 'ket' because they were not good for them.

Most of the streets in the ancient part of York are called 'gates'. They are named not from the four medieval gateways, which are actually called bars, but from the Viking word 'Gata' meaning 'road' or 'way'. Many of the street-names in York give clues to the city's Viking past. York was of course the base for the Viking kings and their presence is remembered in the name of Coney Street, which means 'King's Street'. Coney derives from the Viking word 'Konungra' meaning 'King'.

There were a number of other Viking street names in York that described the Viking people who once lived there. Some of these streets no longer exist today. One of these lost streets was called Hartergate a street that belonged to a Viking called Hjartar. The street of Goodramgate is however still in existence. It is named after a Viking called Guthrum.

Common Viking elements in the place-names of Northern England

Airg: Irish word for shieling or shelter imported into Britain by the Vikings.

Beck: from the Old Norse 'Bekkr' meaning 'stream'.

Berge: a hill, but not to be confused with the Anglo-Saxon word Burgh meaning a fortified manor.

By: a farm or village often Danish and usually found at the end of a name like Whitby.

Fell: from the viking word 'Fjall' for a high mountain, such as Cross Fell in the Pennines.

Force: from the Viking word 'foss' meaning waterfall.

Dale: from the Viking word Dalr, but a word that became widely used in English.

Garth: a Viking word for a yard or enclosure.

Gata: means 'road or way'. It often occurs as 'gate' in the oldest street names of historic northern towns and cities, but it is by no means exclusive to Viking settled areas.

Gill: Viking word for a small ravine.

Holm: from the Viking 'Holmr' meaning water meadow, island or flat land surrounded by a stream, river, or other water feature.

Karl: a peasant or churl, occurs in names like Carlton, probably a Viking adaptation of the Anglo-Saxon place-name Charlton.

Kirk: Viking word for a church, but also the northern Anglo-Saxon form of church.

Ker: a marsh or poor quality land.

Scale: Viking word for a shelter or shieling.

Staith: a dwelling place found in names like Staithes on the Yorkshire coast or Croxteth, Merseyside.

Thwaite: a Viking meadow or clearing.

Thorpe: Viking for a small farm, hamlet or outlying settlement.

Toft: a building plot or farm.

Wath: from the Viking word Vath, a ford across a river or stream.

A particularly interesting street name in York that gives a clue to a people of a particular ethnic origin is the street of Jubbergate. It is thought that this street is named after Jews who settled in the area. However these Jews did not arrive until well after the Viking period. In Viking times Jubbergate was called Brettegate and lay just outside the city walls. The name meant 'Street of the Britons' and is thought to refer to Welsh speaking Cumbrians who were captured or employed by Norwegian Vikings and brought to York, perhaps to serve as Viking slaves or servants. Alternatively these Britons may have been employed as fighters in the Viking army. It is likely that they intermarried with the Vikings in York.

Some of York's Viking street-names indicate the occupations of the Vikings who once lived and worked there. Coppergate, where major excavations of a Viking settlement have been undertaken, gets its name from the Viking 'Kopparigat' meaning street of the joiners, turners or coopers. Other streets that indicate the employment of their former occupants include Fishergate and Skeldergate.

The Viking street name Skeldergate means 'street of the shield makers'. York's Hundgate was the street where Vikings kept their hounds and this street name occurs in other northern towns like Darlington. York also once had a street called Ketmongergate. This was a Viking name that meant 'street of the flesh seller'.

Viking Place-names in Yorkshire

Ainderby Quernhow: Eindrithi's farm. Quernhow is from the Old Norse 'Kvern-Howe' a 'mill stone hill'.

Aireyholme: From Erghum. This shows Irish Viking influence and means 'the shielings'.

Askrigg: Name means 'ash tree ridge'. The Spelling of ash is due to Viking influence.

Aysgarth: Derives from 'Ayks kerth' meaning 'hill gap where oaks grew'.

Beckwithshaw: From the Viking 'Beck-Vith' meaning stream-wood. 'Shaw' is Anglo-Saxon for a wood.

Carperby: From an Old Norse-Irish personal name Caiperes.

Cleckheaton: Heaton is from the Anglo-Saxon 'high farm'. Cleck is from the Old Norse 'Klakr' a lumpy hill.

Danby: Village of the Danes.

Faceby: Feitr's by, a Viking name meaning 'fat person's village'.

Flambororough Head: The fort belonging to a Viking called Fleinn.

Fridaythorpe: The Thorpe or farm belonging to a Viking called Frigdaeg.

Giggleswick: Gigel's farm or village.

Goathland: Near Whitby means Goda's land.

Grimston: Means 'farm belonging to Grim'. Ton is a Saxon word and Grim is a Viking personal name.

Gunnerside: Gunnar's slope.

Hornby: Hornbothi's farm.

Keld: A spring.

Maltby: Malti's farm.

Melsonby: Melsuithan's Farm or village. A mixed Viking-Irish name.

Mickleby: The large farm or village.

Normanton: The Norseman's settlement.

Osgoodby: Place belonging to Osgood.

Romanby: Place-name belonging to Romund. It has nothing to do with the Romans.

Scarborough: A Viking place-name in Yorkshire that is mentioned in Viking sagas. In the 'Kormakssaga' Scarborough is called Skarthborg and was founded by two Viking brothers called Thorgils and Kormak. Thorgils was known to his brother by the nickname 'Hare Lip', or 'Skarthi'.

Selby: Means the willow farm.

Skipton: Viking influenced form of an Anglo-Saxon place-name Shipton. Means 'sheep farm'.

Sowerby: Means 'muddy farm'.

Wetherby: Farm of the wether - a castrated ram.

Whitby: Hviti's settlement.

Yockenthwaite: The meadow belonging to an Irish Viking called Eogan.

Part Five:
The Norse North West

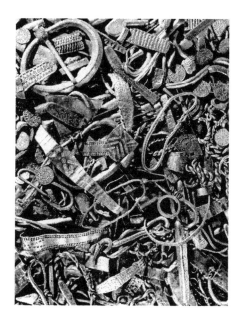

*The Cuerdale Viking hoard. Discovered near Preston in Lancashire
in the nineteenth century*

Part Five :
The Norse North West

Vikings in the North West

Most of Viking Yorkshire had been dominated by the settlement of the Danes, although the northern Yorkshire Dales saw considerable Norwegian settlement. Things begin to change as we continue further west into Cumbria, where the influence of Norwegian settlement is much more apparent. It is also very obvious on the Isle of Man, only forty miles off the Cumbrian coast.

In central and eastern Lancashire Viking place-names are not as obvious as they are in central Yorkshire or the Lake District. There is some Danish influence in the easterly parts of Lancashire, probably associated with settlements from Yorkshire, but the most significant area of Viking settlement is along the western Lancashire coast, overlooking the Irish Sea. Here we find much evidence for Norwegian settlement with many Viking place-names. They are especially apparent in the area around Liverpool and continue across the other side of the Mersey into the Wirral peninsula, which formerly lay within the county of Cheshire.

The Norwegians dominated the Irish Sea from their great colony at Dublin. Norwegian settlements in Cumbria, Lancashire, the Isle of Man, northern Wales, the Scottish Isles and parts of the Irish coast were all associated with the Dublin colony, where there may also have been some Danish influence.

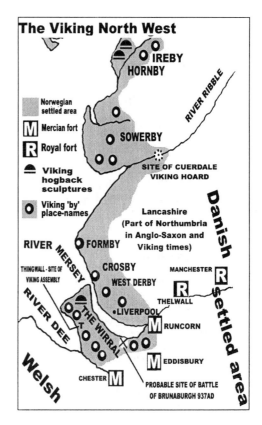

Viking Lancashire.

Norwegians in Cumbria

We have already mentioned in an earlier section of this book that Cumbria was a stronghold of the Britons and was a region where there was considerable Welsh Celtic influence. Danish or Anglo-Saxon influence wasn't as strong in Cumbria as it was in Yorkshire. However, the lakes and mountains of Cumbria were a very attractive place of settlement for the Norwegians. Evidence for Norwegian settlement in this particular county of the north is greater than that of any other part of England.

Place-names of Norwegian origin are found everywhere in Cumbria. Most noticeable are the 'Thwaites'. These are Viking 'meadows or clearings' and appear in names like Bassenthwaite, Applethwaite, Legburthwaite, Branthwaite and Thornthwaite. Then we have the Viking 'Scales', - equivalent to the Anglo-Saxon word 'Shiel' meaning 'Shelter'. Cumbrian examples of this Viking place-name include Winscale, Seascales, Deanscales, and Scales.

Seeking Shelters

Norwegians called shelters 'Scales', but Irish-Norwegians also used the Irish term 'airg' which shows up in places like Eryholme, Airyholme or Airy Hill in Yorkshire. Lancashire place-names like Goosnargh and Grimsargh in the Ribble Valley also recall this word.

Water features often have Viking names in Cumbria. For example fords across rivers were called 'waths', a Viking word that occurs in place-names like Stockdalewath. Waterfalls in Cumbria are called 'forces' while streams are called 'becks'. These are also words of Viking origin. Norwegian place-names in Cumbria suggest that many Norwegians had already settled in Cumbria before Irish-Norwegians came to settle here from Dublin after 918 AD.

Danes seem to have been present in some parts of Cumbria and this is most noticeable in the lowland areas formed by the River Eden and along the coastal plain. Here they are apparent in names like Appleby, Hunsonby, Langwathby, Ousby and Lazonby. These names continue north into neighbouring Dumfriesshire in Scotland, where we find Lockerbie, Middlebie and Canonbie. The Danish settlers of Yorkshire and Lancashire could have easily entered Cumbria via the Eden valley and gradually colonised Westmorland, Cumberland and southern Dumfriesshire. However it is worth considering the possibility that Norwegians gave Danish style names to settlements established in lowland areas. Place-names ending in 'by' were not exclusive to the Danes, especially in Britain where Danes and Norwegians were in close contact. In fact place-names ending in 'by' often show Norwegian influence and this is particularly the case with a large number of 'by' place-names in the Wirral peninsula of the Merseyside region.

Forces and Linns

In Cumbria, Teesdale and Yorkshire waterfalls are called 'Forces' from the Viking word 'fors'. In the County Durham valley of Weardale and in Northumberland waterfalls are called 'Linns' - a Celtic word adopted by the Anglo-Saxons. Examples include Hareshaw Linn in Tynedale and High Force in Teesdale.

Norsemen in the North West

When the Irish-Norwegians were evicted from Dublin in 918 AD they took to their boats to seek land across the Irish Sea. They settled in places where there was a substantial colony of Danes or Norwegians, in areas like Cumbria, the Ribble valley, the Wirral and Merseyside. Near Liverpool they established the settlements of Croxteth and Toxteth.

Liverpool's name may date from this period, perhaps deriving from the Old Norse 'Lifrig Pol' - or 'muddy creek'. The River Mersey was close to the southern edge of Viking settlement but place-names around the Mersey suggest that there was significant Viking settlement around the Mersey estuary.

Further north, towards Preston, the Ribble valley was part of a Viking trade route between Dublin and York. Around the year 905 AD one group of Vikings travelling this route dumped and buried a hoard of 1,300 Viking items in the riverbank at Cuerdale near Preston. They never returned to recover their hidden treasure and the hoard was not discovered until the nineteenth century.

To the north of the Ribble, the county of Lancashire narrows into a strip of land bordered by Yorkshire on the east and Cumbria to the north. A scattering of Viking names exist in this vicinity around Blackpool, Morecambe and Lancaster where names like Westby, Nateby, Goosnargh, Dolphinholme, Torrisholme and Hawthornthwaite can be found. In the coastal region at Heysham and Bolton-le-Sands Viking hogback sculptures have been found.

> ## Liverpool Norwegians and Manchester Danes
>
> Norwegians tended to settle in the west of Lancashire near Liverpool, where they had arrived from Ireland. Danes were found in the east of Lancashire around Manchester where they had arrived from Yorkshire. This was the fringe of Danish settlement and is characterised by place-names like Urmston, Hulm (holm), and Oldham - formerly Aldholm. Manchester was part of Viking Northumbria but it also lay very close to the border with Anglo-Saxon Mercia. The neighbouring county of Cheshire was situated in Mercia. This meant that Manchester had a strategic location. Manchester was captured and brought under the control of the Anglo-Saxon king Edward the Elder. In the year 919 AD, Edward fortified Manchester against the Vikings of the North. So in Anglo-Saxon times, Manchester was a fortress that defended the midlands against the men of the north.

Like Yorkshire, Lancashire was divided into 'wappentakes' or Viking administrative districts and these survived for many centuries. However, on the whole, Viking settlement in Lancashire seems to be characterised by isolated pockets of dense Viking settlement and areas where they seem to have been thin on the ground. This is especially noticeable when compared to the dense and evenly spread concentration of Viking place-names in neighbouring Cumbria. It is also noticeable that Lancashire also tends to use the Midland and southern English word 'Brook' for a stream whilst Yorkshire and Cumbria use the Viking word 'Beck'.

Norsemen of Merseyside and the Wirral

Most of the old county of Cheshire, in what was then western Mercia, lay outside the sphere of Viking influence, although there was slight Danish influence in the north and east towards Manchester where we find place-names like Knutsford (Canute's Ford), Cheadle Hulme, Kettleshulme and Toft.

However, the most important area of Viking settlement in Cheshire was undoubtedly the Wirral peninsula - an area that is now part of Merseyside.

The Viking battle of the Wirral

It is thought that one of the most important battles ever fought between the Anglo-Saxons and the Vikings was fought on the Wirral. This was the battle of Brunaburh fought in 937 AD somewhere in the North West of England. The site of the battle has never been identified, but the most likely location is Bromborough, near the banks of the Mersey and within the Wirral peninsula. The Scots assisted the Vikings in this battle, but it was the Anglo-Saxons under the leadership of King Athelstan who were victorious. The victory limited the threat of Viking expansion in the north of England.

The Wirral formed the far north western corner of the historical county of Cheshire and is situated on the coast between the River Mersey and the River Dee. It is sandwiched between the city of Liverpool and the coast of north Wales.

It is known from historical records that an Irish-Norse Viking called Ingimund settled the Wirral. He was one of a group of many Irish-Norwegians to be evicted from Ireland around 920 AD and he was among the first wave of Irish Norwegians to settle in the Merseyside area. Many more Vikings would follow.

Scouse- An Irish-Norse Dialect?

It is possible that Merseyside's Scouse dialect and the dialect of the Wirral may have some Irish-Norse roots. Scouse pronunciations like "Doze Tings Dere" (Those Things There) also occur in the Viking settled Shetlands and Orkneys where they are known to be of Norse origin. This kind of pronunciation also occurs in Dublin. It is usually assumed that Irish immigration in recent centuries most greatly affected the dialect of Merseyside. Nevertheless there is much evidence for significant Irish-Norse settlement in the whole Merseyside area. The Scandinavian connection continues into modern times. By shear coincidence it was eighteenth century Scandinavian sailors who introduced a stew or broth to the area that was known as 'lapskaus' or 'lobscouse'. It became especially popular amongst the Liverpudlian sailors who came to be known as 'lobscousers' and later 'Scousers'. The name is now given to anyone originating from Liverpool

---

There is much place-name evidence for Viking settlement in the Wirral where we find names like Thurstaston, Greasby, Whitby, Raby, Pensby and Irby. The last of these place-names means 'settlement of the Irish Vikings'. In fact the Wirral was a small Viking State in its own right, with a local parliament held at Thingwall, a place-name near Heswall on the south side of the peninsula. Thingwall's name derives from the Viking word 'Thingvollr' meaning 'the Assembly Field'. There is much folklore to associate the Wirral with the Vikings and at least one expert believes that the Norse language continued to be spoken in the Wirral for centuries after the Norman Conquest.

> **Chester City and the Irish Vikings**
>
> If the Vikings of the Wirral posed a threat to the neighbouring countryside than the Mercian City of Chester must have played an important defensive role. This Anglo-Saxon City lay close to the north eastern border of Wales, but was also situated on the neck of the Wirral peninsula, with the Irish Vikings of the Wirral located to its north. When we consider that Danes were also not far away in Lancashire to the north, we can see why Anglo-Saxon kings in the south recognised Chester's important defensive role.
>
> However, the Vikings were not unwelcome in the city of Chester, as it is known that a small community of Irish-Vikings lived in the city in Viking times. They lived in a street close to a bridge over the River Dee.
>
> To the west of Chester, the coast of North Wales also came under strong Irish-Norse influence as is shown by names like 'Great Orme's Head'. This may account for some of the similarities between the accents of Chester, Liverpool and North Wales that are still apparent today.

Vikings in the Isle of Man

One area of Britain that was very strongly affected by Viking settlement was the Isle of Man. Until the middle of the ninth century AD, the Isle of Man was inhabited by Celts, who spoke Manx, a Gaelic type of language. In fact this language was still widely spoken on the island as late as the nineteenth century. The last native speaker of Manx died in 1974, but the language is still taught on this island to this day. The language is fundamentally Gaelic, but shows strong Viking influence.

The Isle of Man escaped the Anglo-Saxon invasions that ravaged the British mainland in the fifth century, but it did not escape the Vikings. From around 800AD the Vikings raided and colonised the island as they had done with other areas around the coasts of the Irish Sea.

> **Orry, the Viking King of Man**
>
> King Orry, a Viking leader of the Isle of Man is widely remembered in the folklore of the Isle of Man. Orry was the Gaelic name of Godred Crovan, a Viking-Scot who ruled the island from 1079 to 1095. When Godred first landed on the island during a clear night the islanders asked him "where was his country of origin?" He pointed to the Milky Way and stated that this was the road to his home country. In Manx, the Milky Way is known as King Orry's road.

The Isle of Man was closely tied to the Irish Viking colony at Dublin and was later tied to the Kingdom of Norway. Norway held possession of the island until 1266 when it was sold to Scotland. In 979 AD the Vikings had established a parliament on the Isle of Man. The Isle of Man's parliament still exists today and is known as the 'Tynwald'. The name derives from the Viking word 'Thingvollr' meaning 'Assembly Field'. It is believed to be the oldest legislative assembly in the world. The Tynwald was originally sited on Tynwald Hill at St John's in the centre of the island. The Viking kingdom of the Isle of Man included the western Isles off the coast of Scotland. Representatives of all these islands were expected to attend the Viking parliamentary meetings held on the Isle of Man.

Place-names on the Isle of Man show a mixture of both Gaelic and Viking names. Gaelic words in the place-names include purt (harbour), cronk (hill) and balla (farm). Viking place-names include Jurby, Ronaldsway, Regaby, Crosby, Garth, Sulby, Ravensdale, Dalby and Colby. Hills and mountains are named fells in Viking fashion with the highest peak being Snaefell.

Viking Place-names in the North West and Cumbria

Aintree: Near Liverpool. From 'eintre' meaning lonely tree.

Ambleside: 'A' Melr Saetr meaning the river sandbank shieling.

Appleby: Farm where apples grew'.

Aspatria: Part Norse place-name. Means St Patrick's Ash Tree.

Bassenthwaite: The clearing belonging to Bastun.

Cartmel: From Kartr-Melr 'the rocky sandbank'.

Clitherhoe: From the Old Norse 'Klithra Haugr' meaning song thrush hill.

Coniston: Combination of Anglo-Saxon ton meaning farm and Viking word Konungr meaning king.

Copeland: From Old Norse 'Kaupa Land' meaning purchased land.

Crosby: Near Liverpool. Means the Viking settlement with a cross.

Croxteth: Near Liverpool, means place belonging to Krokr.

Formby: Forni's farm.

Grimsargh: Irish Viking shieling belonging to Grim.

Goosnargh: Irish Viking shieling belonging to Gosan.

Keswick: Means cheese wick, a cheese farm. The hard K sound is due to Viking influence.

Kirkby: Place with church.

Knutsford: A ford belonging to a Scandinavian called Canute, but probably not King Canute.

Langwathby: The Long Ford Farm.

Liverpool: Possibly from the Norse Lifra, a stream with thick water.

Oldham: Originally Ald Holmr. The old water meadow.

Ormskirk: The church belonging to Orm.

Roby: Place near Liverpool. Means boundary farm.

Sedbergh: Flat topped hill. It has the same meaning as Sadberge near Darlington.

Sescale: Shielings or shelters near the sea.

Skelmersdale: Now a new town. Original settlement simply meant valley belonging to Skelmer.

Thingwall: From 'Thingvollr' - the site of a Viking assembly on the Wirral.

Toxteth: Near Liverpool. Means Toki's place.

Tranmere: From Viking word 'Trani' meaning crane (a bird) and Melr meaning sandbank.

Whitby: Near Ellesmere Port. Means White farm.

Part Six:
North East Angle Land

*Lewis Carroll's Jabberwocky was almost certainly inspired
by a County Durham dragon legend with
Anglo-Saxon or Viking origins.*

probably descendants of the old Anglo-Saxon Kings of Northumbria and were virtual kings in the North-East.

The people of the Bernician Earldom, which stretched from the Tees to the Firth of Firth, were undoubtedly Angles, but Irish based historians of the time ignored the difference between Angles and Saxons and called Bernicia 'North Saxonland'. This was their way of distinguishing Bernicia from the Viking parts of Northern England and from the 'South Saxon Land' of Alfred the Great in the south of England.

Part Six :
North East Angle Land

Vikings in Bernicia - The North East of England

The boundary of the Danelaw ran from the River Thames roughly to the River Dee at Chester in North West England. This divided the Anglo-Saxon territory in the south of England from the Viking territory of the north. This division is very well known and often mentioned by historians, but they often fail to mention that there was another lesser known division in the north of England, along the River Tees.

The Murder of Eric Bloodaxe

Oswulf, the Earl or High Reeve of Bamburgh who ruled Bernicia north of the River Tees, is thought to have been one of the men behind the plot that resulted in the murder of Eric Bloodaxe. Bloodaxe was the powerful Viking King of Norway and York who was killed in an ambush in 954 AD while crossing the Stainmore Pass in the Teesdale region.

Bernicia lay outside the usual sphere of both Saxon and Viking influence. Its rulers were expected to answer to the Viking Kings of York or to the Saxon Kings of the South, but in practice they were quite independent.

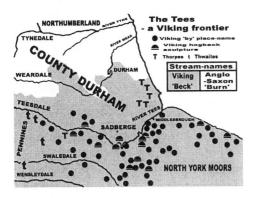

The Tees – a Viking Frontier.

North of the River Tees lay Bernicia, a region that remained Anglo-Saxon or more specifically Angle territory even after the Viking invasion of England. Bernicia came under the rule of the Angle High Reeves, or Earls of Bamburgh. These High Reeves were

More Vikings in Norfolk than Northumberland?

It is not just history that tells us that Bernicia lay largely outside the influence of the Vikings of York. Place-names show an astonishing lack of Viking influence in Northumberland and Durham compared to the other northern counties of Yorkshire, Lancashire and Cumbria.

Vikings are usually associated with northern England, but the east midland counties of Lincolnshire, Leicestershire and Derbyshire show much stronger Danish influence in their place-names than Northumberland and Durham. The most southerly collection of Danish names is in East Anglia in the county of Norfolk. Norfolk shows particularly strong traces of Viking settlement in the Great Yarmouth area, where we find place-names like Ormesby, Thrigby, Mautby, Thorpe, Hemsby, Ashby, Filby, Kirby, Lowestoft, Thwaite, Rollesby, Clippesby, Stokesby, Billockby, Aldeby. Most of these names lie within a large 'island' of land bordered by the rivers Thurne and Yare. Other parts of the south saw some Viking settlement as far south as the River Thames, but these are less frequent and nowhere near as dense as in Norfolk, which was one of the first places to be invaded and settled by the Danes.

I mention Norfolk because there is a tendency to think of the North and particularly the North East as being a Viking settled region, while the south is often perceived as being free of Vikings. When we compare place-names in Norfolk to place-names in Northumberland we discover that the reverse is sometimes the case. Norfolk even uses the Viking word 'beck' for a stream compared to Northumberland where the old Anglo-Saxon word 'burn' is used.

Vikings of Teesside

Most Viking place-names in the North East region are situated along the River Tees. In other words they are found in the very south of the region near the border with Yorkshire. Viking place-names along the Tees include the village of Aislaby on the Tees near Yarm. Its name means 'Aislac's farm'. There are also a handful of place-names ending in 'Thorpe' in this particular area.

Names ending in 'by' or 'thorpe' are Danish words for a farm, village or outlying settlement. These Viking names are found everywhere in Yorkshire. Look at a map of North Yorkshire and you find dozens of them - Hornby, Girsby, Whitby, Swainby, Faceby, Danby, Huby, Asenby, Brandsby and so on. Look at a comparative map of Northumberland and you will not find any. County Durham lies between Northumberland and Yorkshire but even here you find only a few Viking place-names. Place-names in Durham and Northumberland are almost overwhelmingly of Angle origin.

The Viking Midlands

The most typical Viking place-names in England are those ending in 'by'. These are found mainly in the midlands and the north and signify the site of a farm or village of Viking origin. They are usually Danish. Many names ending in 'by' are located around five major towns in the East Midlands that are known to Viking historians as the 'Five Boroughs' of the Danelaw. The five boroughs were Lincoln, Nottingham, Leicester, Derby and Stamford. These were important Anglo-Saxon towns that were seized from the Mercians by the Vikings and made into important centres of Viking trade and administration. The counties attached to these towns have a high proportion of Viking place-names. Lincolnshire has one of the largest number of Danish place-names in England where examples include Utterby, Grimsby, Markby, Fulletby, Ashby, Claxby, Raithby, Hundleby, Orby and Revesby. In Leicestershire examples include find Beeby, Lowesby, Barsby, Kilby, Arnesby and Shearsby.

Because of the scarcity of Viking place-names in the North East it is worth searching to find them. The first place to look for Viking place-names is along the River Tees where they are relatively easy to find. It is possible to regard the Tees as the north eastern boundary of Viking settlement in England. However, as with the Mersey (the south western border of Viking settlement) we find substantial evidence for Viking settlement in this 'border region'.

Many former Viking settlements along the River Tees were swallowed up by the growth of industrial Middlesbrough and Teesside in the nineteenth century, so we should not be fooled into thinking they belong to the industrial age. Viking place-names in Teesside include places like Thornaby, Maltby, Lackenby, Lazenby, Ingleby Barwick, Tollesby, Stainsby, Normanby, Coulby Newham and Ormesby.

These places are all on the southern side of the River Tees in an area that was historically in Yorkshire. Apart from Aislaby, a little further upstream, no 'by' names of this kind can be found on the north side of the river near Stockton and Hartlepool where the river is widest. This is because the places on the south side of the Tees were part of the old Viking Kingdom of Jorvik. Those on the north side of the Tees lay within Bernicia.

Further up the valley of the Tees, we find several other Viking place-names like Girsby, Selaby, Cleasby, Eppleby and Killerby. Here, where the river is narrower, the Viking names are found on both sides of the river in both County Durham and Yorkshire. However on the Durham side, they are rarely found far from the River Tees. One very interesting place-name in the Teesdale area is Raby Castle. This is in County Durham and is a good four miles to the north of the Tees. Part of the castle dates from the late Viking period and is thought to have been the site of a mansion belonging to Canute, the Danish King of England. He is certainly recorded as owning a mansion near Staindrop, and this is the village right next to the castle. The Viking name Raby may mean 'boundary settlement' or 'settlement with roe deer'. Interestingly there is also a place called Raby on the Wirral in North West England.

In the middle section of the Tees valley near Darlington we find a place called Sockburn. The name Sockburn is a corruption of a more ancient name Soca Burgh. It lies in a huge meander of the river Tees. Bishops of Lindisfarne and York were consecrated here in Anglo-Saxon times, but in Viking times it became a major centre for the carving of Viking sculptures. A number of distinctive Viking carvings called Hogbacks have been found here.

A few miles to the north of Sockburn, along an old Roman road lies the village of Sadberge about half way between Stockton and Darlington. Sadberge, which has a Viking name, was the capital of the only Viking 'wappentake' north of the Tees. A Wappentake was a Viking 'council' or administrative district where the affairs of the local district were settled. The wappentake stretched along the northern bank of the River Tees from Hartlepool to Teesdale and was possibly an outlying part of the Kingdom of

Jorvik. The Danes or Norwegians may have temporarily seized this land from Bernicia. There are certainly records of Vikings owning land on the immediate north bank of the Tees.

The Origin of County Durham

In 875 AD, the Community of St Cuthbert fled from the Holy Island of Lindisfarne to escape the continuous Viking invasion of the North. The community was a powerful and highly influential collection of monks under the leadership of the Bishop of Lindisfarne. Their main concern was in protecting the coffin and relics of the seventh century Northumbrian saint, Cuthbert, whose remains were held with great reverence in the north.

For seven years the community wandered the north, settling for short periods at various sites across the region like Norham on Tweed and Carlisle. In 882AD the community supported the claims of the Danish leader Guthred to the Kingdom of York. In return for their support he granted the community land in southern Bernicia, between the Rivers Tyne and Tees. These lands were centred upon the town of Conecaster on the River Wear. Conecaster is known today as Chester-le-Street. An Anglo-Saxon 'minster' or cathedral was built at Conecaster and the surrounding lands were the first stage in the development of what would become County Durham.

The land was known as Haliwerfolklond or St Cuthbert's land and although it was part of Bernicia it was effectively a buffer region between the Yorkshire Vikings and the Angles of northern Bernicia. Positioning the community in southern Bernicia may have been a strategic move by Guthred. It would help to discourage Bernician raids on Danish settlements in Yorkshire and the Tees valley. It also discouraged Scottish raids or fresh Viking raids from Scandinavia in the North East. By 995 such raids had forced the Cuthbert community to move to a new, naturally defended site on the River Wear called 'Dun Holm' which has an Anglo-Viking name meaning 'hill-island'. We know this site today as Durham. In Norman times Durham became the capital of the Prince Bishops. They inherited their combined political and ecclesiastical powers from the Earls of Bamburgh and Bishops of Lindisfarne.

Scula and Olaf the Vikings of Durham

When the evicted Irish-Norwegians from Dublin crossed the Irish Sea in 918 under the leadership of King Ragnald they seized the city of York from the Danes. Ragnald appointed himself as ruler of the North after fighting two great battles at Corbridge on Tyne. It is known that Irish-Norsemen settled in the Wirral and there are traces of Irish Viking settlement in Cumbria and North Yorkshire. Ragnald looked for land to offer as a prize for his military supporters and took Bernician territory in south and east Durham. He seized land from the Bishop of Chester-le-Street (the predecessor of the Bishop of Durham) and gave it to his warrior generals called Scula and Olaf Ball. It is thought that these men shared the land out amongst their Irish-Viking followers. Scula was given land in the south of the bishop's territory, at Billingham and at School Aycliffe (Scula's Aycliffe) near Darlington, Olaf Ball received the whole eastern coast from Hartlepool to Sunderland.

Worm Legends in Durham - a Viking Myth?

The famous worm legends of County Durham are often associated with the Vikings. In some Germanic languages a 'Wyrm' was a wyvern or dragon. In Scandinavia dragons were called 'Orms'. In the North-East it is sometimes thought that the worm legends recall long forgotten battles between Anglo-Saxons and Vikings. Today most people in the North East region know the ancient Lambton Worm legend. The Lambton Worm is said to have lived near the River Wear in medieval times and terrorised the area between Sunderland and Chester-le-Street. It was made popular by a music hall song in the nineteenth century.

Whist Lads haad yer gobs
Aa'll tell ye aal an aaful story
Whist Lads haad yer gobs
Aal tell ye aboot the Worm

Historically the Sockburn Worm legend of the River Tees was more famous. It was apparently slain by Sir John Conyers using his sword known as the Conyers falchion. The sword is now in Durham Cathedral. Conyers belonged to a Norman family but the legend is thought to predate the Conquest. The handle of the sword dates from the late Viking period and incorporates the emblem of a Northumbrian earl. Perhaps Conyers took false credit for a more ancient victory.

The Sockburn Worm legend inspired Lewis Caroll, who lived nearby, to write his Jabberwocky poem. The falchion that killed the beast has been presented for centuries to each new Bishop of Durham on the bridge at Croft on Tees near Darlington on the borders of Durham and Yorkshire. Lewis Carroll's childhood home overlooks this bridge where part of the Jabberwocky was penned. It is worth recalling his famous poem, as it portrays a battle between a man and a dragon in a way in which the Anglo-Saxons and Norse mythologists of ancient times would surely have approved.

The Jabberwocky

A Viking Worm Legend?

'Twas brillig, and the slithy toves
Did gyre and gimble in the wabe:
All mimsy were the borogroves
And the mome raths outgrabe.

"Beware the Jabberwock, my son!
The jaws that bite, the claws that catch!
Beware the Jubjub bird and shun
The frumious Bandersnatch!"

He took his vorpal sword in hand:
Long time the manxome foe he sought-
So rested he by the Tumtum tree,
And stood a while in thought.

And as in uffish thought he stood,
The Jabberwock
with eyes of flame,
Came whiffling through
the tulgey wood
And burbled as it came!

One two! One two!
And through and through
The vorpal blade went
snicker snack!
He left it dead, and with its head
He went galumphing back.

"And hast thou slain
the Jabberwock
Come to me my breamish boy !
O' frabjuous day
Callooh ! Callay !"
He chortled in his joy.

Vikings of Tyneside and Northumberland

A small scattering of Viking place-names can be found throughout County Durham, particularly along the Durham coast. However, once we reach Tyneside on the border of Northumberland and Durham, it is much harder to find Viking place-names than it was around Teesside on the Yorkshire border. The only place-name ending with the typical Danish 'by' in the Tyneside area is Follingsby near Gateshead. This is a doubtful name because the earliest spellings only date to the 12th century and suggest a derivation from 'Folet' an Old French word for a 'fool'.

Two other prominent Tyneside place-names with possible Viking origins are Byker and Walker. The Viking word 'Ker' means 'poor land or marsh'. It suggests that the Vikings had to make do with poor quality land on Tyneside. Walker is named from its proximity to Hadrian's Wall. It means 'wall-marsh'. However the word 'Ker' was widespread in northern English after Viking times, so Byker and Walker may not be Viking settlements at all.

One area of Tyneside known to have come under Danish influence was Tynemouth, where the Danish leader Halfdene established a stronghold on a hill overlooking the Tyne in 875 AD. Viking influence survived at Tynemouth for centuries, as Scandinavian personal names were unusually numerous amongst the population here in the years after 1066.

In later centuries dialect experts observed that Tynemouth's dialect was closer to the dialects of Sunderland, South Shields and the Durham coast than the dialect of neighbouring Northumberland or Tyneside. This dialect similarity is not apparent today, but interestingly, the Durham coast, like Tynemouth, was an area of Viking settlement.

Evidence for Viking settlement in Northumberland is scant, although there are traces of Viking place-names in south east Northumberland, as well as in parts of Coquetdale and the Tyne Valley. There is some noticeable Viking influence in the parts of Northumberland that share their border with neighbouring Cumbria. However the place-name evidence for Viking settlement in Northumberland is much lower than that of any other northern English county.

'Gan Yem' - or 'Going Home' a Tyneside Viking phrase?

The Tyneside phrase 'gan yem' which means 'going home' can still be understood by Scandinavians today. Gan Yem is however also a very significant aspect of the Cumbrian dialect and may have originated there and spread into neighbouring Northumberland or Durham. Miners often originated in the neighbouring rural areas and may also have brought dialect words into Tyneside. Mining terms like 'skeets' and 'marra' are sometimes thought to have Old Norse origins.

Tees 'Becks' and Tyne 'Burns'

Stream names in the North East demonstrate that dialect and place-names are closely related and may hold clues to our Anglo-Viking origins. According to the Ordnance Survey maps, County Durham is the border zone for Burns and Becks. In the north of the County, the Anglo-Saxon word 'Burn' is used for a stream, but in the south of the county the

Viking word 'Beck' is used. I believe that the term 'beck' is also used in the east of the county as far north as Sunderland, although the maps insist that the word 'burn' should be used here.

In Northumberland and Tyneside the Anglo-Saxon word 'burn' is used. Northumberland's only beck, the River Wansbeck, is a misnomer as it actually derives from the Anglo-Saxon 'Wagon's Spic' meaning Wagon Bridge. Nearly all the streams that join the Tees are Becks and all the streams that join the Tyne are Burns. Along the Wear there are mixtures of the two, especially between Weardale and Durham City. Occasionally in lower Weardale streams are called Burn-Becks. These include the Bed-burn Beck in Hamsterley Forest.

The Viking term Beck is used for streams in North Yorkshire, Cumbria, Lincolnshire, Norfolk, northern Lancashire and even in parts of Dumfriesshire. However, most of Scotland uses the Anglo-Saxon word Burn. The word Brook is used for streams in most southern parts of England and may have entered the language at a later date. It may have replaced the older word 'burn' or 'bourn'. Burn or Bourn is not used for streams in the midlands or the south, but it has survived in place-names like Sherbourne. It is thought that 'brook' was an old word that originally meant marsh, but was later used for a stream. It is used in the Midlands and southern England including Suffolk.

In the north the word brook is used in most of Lancashire, Derbyshire and in southerly parts of Yorkshire around Sheffield and Huddersfield. Interestingly these correspond to areas where the Mercian dialect seems to have had a stronger influence than Northumbrian in ancient times. In general, Yorkshire uses the word beck. The word Stream is of course known to everyone but is used in the south west of England instead of Brook.

Viking Place-names in the North East

Aislaby: On the Tees. Means the farm belonging to Aslac.
Ayresome: Teesside. From the Old Norse 'ar husum' meaning the river houses.
Balder: A Norse God and a river in Teesdale. The Yorkshire place-name Baldersby belonged to a Viking settler called Balder.
Byker: A rare Viking place-name on Tyneside meaning place near a marsh.
Crook: In Weardale, County Durham. From a Viking word meaning river bend.
Greta: Viking river name near Barnard Castle in Teesdale meaning stony stream.
High Force: A Teesdale waterfall. Force was the Viking word for a waterfall.
Ireshopeburn: Anglo-Saxon meaning, valley-stream belonging to the Irish, probably Irish Vikings from Cumbria, found in Weardale.
Lackenby: Near Middlesbrough - belonged to a Viking called Hlackande.
Lazenby: A Viking place-name in Teesside that means the village belonging to a Leysingr or freeman.
Marske: From a Viking pronunciation of the word marsh.
Normanby: Teesside place-name meaning village of the Norseman.
Ormesby: Near Middlesbrough. Means Orm's farm.
Raby Castle: Teesdale castle with Danish name meaning roe deer or boundary farm.
School Aycliffe: Near Darlington. Named after an Irish-Viking General called Scula.
Thornaby: Teesside place-name meaning Thormad's farm.
Thorpe Thewles: From the Viking word 'thorpe' meaning a farm and the Medieval English word Thewles meaning immoral.

Dialect in the North East - Anglo-Saxon or Viking?

One of the most puzzling aspects of the North Eastern region is its dialect. It is popularly assumed that the North East dialect traces its origins back to the Vikings. It is often stated that Vikings extensively settled in the 'North East' and that 'Northumbria' was England's most important area of Viking settlement. However, it has been demonstrated in this chapter that we need to clarify what is meant by 'Northumbria' and what constitutes the 'North East'.

In many history books references to the extensive settlement of Vikings in 'Northumbria' or the 'North East' should be treated cautiously since they are usually referring to the Yorkshire area rather than the North East as we know it today. The view that the North East or Northumbria region saw extensive Viking settlement has coloured the popular view that the dialect of Northumberland and Durham is a 'Norse' dialect.

The idea of the North East's dialect being Viking is often backed up by stories of Geordies being understood by non-English speaking Norwegians and Danes. Undoubtedly Geordies share a number of dialect words with Scandinavian speakers, but this is by no means unique to the speech of the North East. Cumbrian and Yorkshire dialect speakers also share many words with the Scandinavians. It is also important to acknowledge that Geordies and other northerners share words with Dutch, Frisians, French and the Anglo-Saxons of more ancient times.

Where words are used in the North Eastern region that are specifically Scandinavian in origin, it is not necessarily proof of Scandinavian settlement in the region. Contact with Scandinavians, Dutch and Germans has taken place for many centuries through coastal trade, particularly in the Tyneside area and this will have had a significant influence over time. It is also significant that the Vikings had settled extensively in surrounding areas - Cumbria, Yorkshire, Westmorland and parts of Scotland. In all of these regions many Viking words will have entered the local dialects. It was also inevitable that many Viking words would enter the English language itself, even in areas of southern England that were well outside the regions of Viking settlement.

It is not just the 'Viking' theory of North East dialect that needs to be challenged. Some studies of dialect in the North East region have attempted to emphasise the Anglo-Saxon or more specifically the 'Angle' nature of the dialect, in an attempt bring it in line with the historical evidence of place-names and political history. In some cases attempts have been made to suggest that Northumbrian is a pure Anglo-Saxon or 'Angle dialect'. This theory should be treated with caution. As with all local English dialects Northumbrian speech has seen many different linguistic influences over time. On the whole dialect is a less reliable indication of a region's Viking or Anglo-Saxon origins than the place-names or historical records of the time.

Part Seven: French Connections – The Normans

The Norman North circa 1086
showing major landowners
and early Norman castles

EDINBURGH
BERWICK

Scotland

NORTHYMBRALAND

Robert
Mowbray
NEWCASTLE

ST. CUTHBERT'S
LAND

Cumberland
(Part of
Scotland)

DURHAM

Bishop of
Durham

Count
Alan
of Brittany

Count
Mortain
RICHMOND

Earl
Hugh

FURNESS

Roger
Poitou

NORTH RIDING

Drogo
Bevrere

AMUNDERNESS

Gilbert
Tison

LANCASTER

Roger
Poitou

EURVICSCIRE
(YORKSHIRE)

Ralph
Mortimer

EAST
RIDING

SKIPSEA

Robert Malet

INTER RIPAM
ET MERSHAM
"BETWEEN
RIBBLE
AND
MERSEY"

Ilbert
Lacy

YORK

William
Percy

Roger
Poitou
PENWORTHAM

**WEST
RIDING**

PONTEFRACT

LINCOLESCIRE
(LINCOLNSHIRE)

GWYNEDD

CHESTER

LINCOLN

*The Norman North circa 1086, showing major landowners
and early Norman castles*

14, 1066, the King was defeated and killed near Hastings. The victorious Norman Army led by William 'the Conqueror' would change the history of Britain forever.

Part Seven:
French Connections – The Normans

The Viking French

In the year 1066 an army of Vikings under the leadership of the Norwegian king Harald Hardrada invaded the North of England. On September 20, 1066, at Fulford Gate near the outskirts of York, the Vikings defeated the Northumbrians in a great battle. York was seized and it seemed that the North's future lay once more in the hands of the Scandinavian lords.

However, Harald Hardrada's Viking victory was short lived. Five days later, Harold Godwinson, the Anglo-Saxon king of England, marched north to successfully defeat Hardrada's Viking army in the battle of Stamford Bridge to the east of York. This would not be the end of the drama, as only four days later, yet another 'Viking' invasion commenced, this time from the south.

This was to be a Viking invasion with a difference. On this occasion, the Vikings in question spoke French, were known as the Normans and came from France. Many were descended from Vikings who had settled in northern France from Scandinavia over one hundred and fifty years earlier.

The exhausted army of the English King marched south from York to meet the Norman invading force, but on October

---

Who were the Normans?

During the ninth century, the Vikings increasingly raided the powerful Christian Kingdom of the Franks. It was a kingdom that included France and Germany and was inhabited by people of mixed Germanic and Gallo-Celtic blood. Under the rule of Charlemagne the Franks dominated Europe and their leader was crowned 'Holy Emperor of Rome'. However, in the years after Charlemagne's death, the Frankish kingdom was weakened by Civil War and the Vikings saw this as an opportunity for raiding and plunder. The Danes worked their way along Frankish rivers like the Seine, raiding as far south as Paris.

Norwegians and Danes settled in northern France from around 840 AD with the heaviest concentration being the Danes around the Seine estuary. Irish-Norwegians also settled in the prominent Cotentin peninsula to the west. Franks, Bretons and continetal Saxons were all defeated attempting to defend these Frankish lands against the Viking raiders. The Franks attempted to buy off or evict the Vikings from the land, but were eventually forced to concede defeat. An extensive tract of land was granted to the Vikings and this territory gradually expanded. It came to be known as Normandy - the land of the 'North-Men'. Over time the Vikings of northern France assimilated with the natives and adopted the French language. This race of battle-hardened people would be the ultimate conquerors of England in 1066.

The Normans gradually imposed their rule on England, although at first the people of the north rebelled. In January 1069 seven hundred Norman soldiers were killed at Durham in a massacre and in the following month a similar incident occurred at York.

William the Conqueror, the Norman king of England sought his revenge in the so-called 'Harrying of the North'. In 1070, he sent north an army, which, it is said, destroyed every farm and building between Durham and York. It is sometimes claimed that the North was severely depopulated as a result of this raiding and there is certainly much evidence to suggest that large areas of the North were laid to waste. However a lot of ground would need to be covered for the Normans to enforce absolute devastation and wipe out the population. It seems likely that many people fled to the hills for safety, returning only when the Normans had completed their destructive work.

Viking Place-Names in Normandy

As the Vikings of France adopted the language of the French, Viking place-names in Normandy increasingly took on French pronunciations and spellings. With careful examination hundreds of Viking place-names can be found in Normandy. Many end in 'ville', a word the Vikings adopted from a Latin word meaning villa. It is likely that the Vikings thought of this as a typical or appropriate name for a settlement in France. Here are some examples of Viking place-names in Normandy.

Barneville: Settled by a Viking called Bjarni.
Caudebec: 'Cold Beck'. This has the same meaning as Kalbaek in Denmark and Caldbeck in Cumbria.
Dieppedale: Means 'deep valley'. This has the same meaning as Deepdale in Cumbria and Yorkshire and Djupidalur in Iceland.
Grainville: Settled by a Viking called Grim.
Emondeville: Settled by a Viking called Amundi.
Eroudville: Settled by a Viking called Harald.
Houlbec: 'Hollow beck'. This has the same meaning as Holbeck in Yorkshire and Holbaek in Denmark.
Ingouville: Settled by a Viking called Ingulfr.
Neville: Settled by a Viking called Njall (Niall).
Lanquetot: From the Viking 'Lang Toft'. A long land plot.
Le Torps: From the Viking word 'Thorpe' a farm.
Miquetuit: From the Viking Micklethwaite - 'the big clearing'.
Omonville: Settled by a Viking called Asmund.
Thouberville: Settled by a Viking called Thobert.
Tougerville: Settled by a Viking called Thorgils.
Touttainville: Settled by a Viking called Thorstein.
Tocqueville: Settled by a Viking called Toki.

Norman Surnames from Viking places

Norman surnames often derive from Viking place-names in Normandy. For example the powerful Neville family originate from a place in France called Neville and this was originally a Viking settlement. Occasionally the Normans gave their surnames to settlements in England. This sometimes meant that 'second hand' Viking place-names were brought to England. For example the place-name Emondeville (Amundi's settlement) gave rise to the Norman surname Amundeville. The Amundeville's came to England and owned land near Darlington at a place that came to be known as Coatham Mundeville. Similarly Bolbec Common in Northumberland takes its name from Norman Barons called the De Bolbecs who owned land here. The De Bolbecs took their name from Bolbec, a Viking place-name in France. A small number of apparently Viking place-names in England may in fact be French. For example the place-name Jolby in North Yorkshire seems to incorporate the French personal name Joel.

Barons from Brittany

As the Normans imposed their rule on the North of England, the Norman language and way of life would have an increasingly profound influence on the nations of England, Scotland and Wales. In the years after 1066, the people with the power in the North were the Norman barons. Many lived in strategically placed castles constructed across the region. These castles dominated the landscape and ensured that the Normans kept control of the whole northern region. At York, the most populous city in the north, the Normans built two castles to further reduce the chances of rebellion.

Not all of the new Barons in the north were Norman French. Some came from other parts of France. A significant number were Bretons from Brittany. Brittany is a region of France with Celtic origins and the Bretons had strong historic links to the

Celtic regions of Cornwall and Devon in England. The arrival of Bretons added yet another Celtic element to the population of Britain.

At Richmond, in North Yorkshire, Count Alan the Red of Brittany held the castle. His land included the whole Honor of Richmond, a huge portion of northern Yorkshire that included Swaledale, Wensleydale and the southern side of Teesdale. Bretons are likely to have been numerous in the population of 'Richmondshire' and the north. Names like Alan, Brian and Conan were especially popular amongst the French Bretons.

Norman Family Names in Yorkshire and Lancashire

After the Norman Conquest, most of the Anglo-Saxon nobility was stripped of its land. It passed into the hands of the Norman barons. Nevertheless evidence suggests that some members of the Anglo-Saxon nobility married into the aristocratic Norman families. However, the power rested firmly in the hands of the Normans.

Throughout the north the lands were shared out amongst the most powerful members of the Norman aristocracy. Some of the most powerful were those who had played a key part in William the Conqueror's invasion of England. The families of men like Henry de Neville, who commanded William the Conqueror's fleet during his invasion of England would gain much land. Indeed the Nevilles would grow to become the most powerful barons in the north of England and were still

holding positions of power as late as the Wars of the Roses in the fifteenth century.

In Yorkshire the great land owning barons of the early Norman period included the Mortimers, Lacys and Percys, all families of French origin. In Craven in the West of Yorkshire, King William the Conqueror gave the land to Roger de Poitou. Roger's land ownership was even greater in the North West. In fact most of Lancashire including Amundernerss and all the land between the Mersey and the Ribble belonged to him.

The origin of Lancashire

Roger De Poitou was a powerful baron who owned Amunderness and all the land between the Mersey and the Ribble in North West England. De Poitou chose the ancient Roman fort of Lancaster as the site of his castle and it was from here that he administered his estates. These estates were divided up amongst other Norman barons and the whole region came to be known as the Honor De Lancastre. It was later known as Lancastreshire and eventually became Lancashire. In the Domesday Book of 1086, most of the land in Lancashire north of the Ribble had been regarded as part and parcel of Yorkshire. The land between the Ribble and Mersey was regarded as a separate entity and was simply described as "Between Ribble and Mersey" in the Domesday Book.

Norman Northumberland and Durham

During the conquest of England, the land north of the Tees was something of a thorn in the side of the Normans. The people of this region were remote and rebellious and had regarded themselves as a separate entity from the Viking settled region of Yorkshire and from Anglo-Saxons of southern England. King William attempted to recognise this situation and made more than one attempt to appoint an earl to rule the land north of the Tees in his name. During the period 1066 to 1069 there were a succession of three Earls of Anglo-Saxon origin entrusted to rule the region in the name of the king.

These Anglo-Saxon earls were succeeded by Robert Comines, the first Norman to be appointed Earl of Northumbria north of the Tees. He marched north with an army of 700 Norman soldiers and seized the well-defended city of Durham from the Northumbrians. However Comines and all but two of his soldiers were massacred in the narrow streets of the city. William then appointed an Anglo-Saxon from Northampton called Waltheof to succeed as earl, but Waltheof became involved in a rebellion and William had him executed.

The king then gave Waltheof's political powers to Walcher of Lorraine, a Frenchman who had been appointed Bishop of Durham. Thus Walcher became a kind of 'Earl Bishop' with both political and ecclesiastical powers. However, Walcher proved to be a weak leader, who could not control the activities of his retainers. Unfortunately, they became involved in the murder of a popular Anglo-Saxon noble called Liulf of Lumley near Chester-le-Street. Walcher agreed to meet with the angry Northumbrians at Gateshead to discuss the incident, but the Bishop was murdered by the mob.

A new Bishop of Durham was appointed called William of St Carileph, but the king gave the Earldom of Northumbria to a Norman called Robert Mowbray. However Mowbray was later given permission to sell his political rights in the area south of the

Tyne to the Bishop of Durham. This area became County Durham. So Carileph became the first 'Prince Bishop' of Durham. The Bishop and his successors would live like virtual Kings in the north for centuries to come.

The cathedral and castle at Durham are an imposing symbol of Norman power in the North.

After selling his political rights south of the Tyne, Mowbray's political powers were now confined to the County of Northumberland north of the Tyne. However, the earl came to be involved in a plot to overthrow King William Rufus. It proved to be a failure. Mowbray was ousted from the post of earl and the king seized the earl's castles at Bamburgh, Newcastle and Tynemouth. The territory north of the Tyne became the king's property and was divided into various liberties and shires. These were so remote that they existed as almost separate entities and were often at the mercy of raiding Scots. People in these areas learned to live by raiding and stealing. Norman barons and landowners entrusted with power in these northern areas of Northumberland were preoccupied with defending the region from the Scots.

The political changes instigated by the Normans in the North East turned the region into a kind of Border zone - a block of land sandwiched between England and Scotland. The region was a sparsely populated and somewhat troubled area. It had been brought under the control of the Normans but it was to some extent left to its own devices. This might help to explain why the Domesday Book of 1086 does not cover the counties of Northumberland and Durham. The border counties of Cumberland and Westmorland were also omitted.

The Normans changed the English Language forever

English Words, French Origins

If you can't think of any words in the English language that are of French origin here is a small selection of the thousands of words that were introduced into English by the French. The English word is given alongside the word as it appeared in the language of 'Old French' as spoken by the Normans. These are not necessarily the same as the words used in the French language of today

Roast (the Old French Rost); **Beef** (Boef); **Romance** (Romanz); **Dinner** (Diner); **Diamond** (Diamant); **Obey** (Obeir); **Courtesy** (Curtesie); **Usual** (Usual); **Study** (Estudie); **Tragedy** (Tragedie); **Poison** (Poison); **Mustard** (Moustarde); **Garment** (Garnement); **Scandal** (Scandale); **Sure** (Seur); **Parliament** (Parlement); **Archer** (Archier); **Safe** (Sauf); **Cream** (Cresme); **Pardon** (Pardun); **Flower** (Flur); **Scarce** (Eschars); **Rage** (Rager); **Royal** (Roial); **Reason** (Reisun); **Virtue** (Vertu); **Army** (Armee); **Natural** (Naturel); **Original** (Original); **Metal** (Metal); **Peasant** (Paisent); **Towel** (Toaille); **Perfect** (Parfit); **Mountain** (Montaigne); **Defend** (Defendre); **Continue** (Continuer); **Saint** (Seint); **Blue** (Bleu); **Salvation** (Sauvacion); **Arrange** (Arangier); **Story** (Estoire); **Temptation** (Tentacion); **Please** (Plaisir); **Preserve** (Preserver); **Salmon** (Saumon); **Spy** (Espie); **Suppose** (Supposer); **Wardrobe** (Garderobe); **Volume** (Volum); **Rhyme** (Rime); **Chair** (Chaire); **Poverty** (Poverte); **Treasurer** (Tresorier); **Guard** (Garde); **Mackerel** (Maquerel); **Buckle** (Boucle); **Dozen** (Dozeine); **Quilt** (Coilte).

The Normans introduced many new words into the English language and the spelling and grammar of the language was completely reformed through Norman influence. Words like 'Hus' pronounced 'Hoos' by Anglo-Saxons and Vikings became 'House' under Norman influence.

By the year 1200 around 10,000 French words had been added to the English vocabulary. So any Anglo-Saxons who wanted to succeed in society would find it necessary to learn French words. Over time the mixed Norse and Anglo-Saxon language of the native English merged with the French of the Normans and this set in motion the development of the English language as we know it today.

Norman Place-Names in Northern England

Although the Normans have had a profound influence on the vocabulary of the English language, their influence on place-names is much less significant than that of the Anglo-Saxons or Vikings. This is probably because Normans were largely an elite minority, a ruling class, who lived in castles or manor houses attached to various rural towns and villages that existed under the Norman feudal system. The Normans rarely established new settlements although they occasionally renamed existing ones.

One instance of an Anglo-Saxon place-name being renamed by the Vikings is the place-name Richmond in North Yorkshire. Richmond derives from the French 'Riche-Monte' meaning 'strong hill'. The Anglo-Saxons had called

Richmond 'Hindrelac' meaning 'the clearing of the hind'. Hindrelac was probably thought to be an unsuitable name for the site of such a prestigious Norman Castle.

A small scattering of place-names showing a Norman origin or influence can be found across Britain and a number can be found in the North. The French word 'Beau' meaning beautiful is one element that often occurs in Norman place-names usually in the context of a country seat or mansion. In County Durham notable examples include Beamish, famed as the site of a museum today, but with an Old French name that can be traced to Norman times. Beamish means 'Beautiful Mansion'. In the same region there are places of Norman origin called Bellasis near Billingham and Durham. This name means 'Beautiful Assize' or 'Beautiful Seat'. In Northumberland, we find Beaufront meaning 'Beautiful Brow' and this is the site of a Medieval Castle. The names may have been chosen by the powerful to emphasise their prestige as much as their beauty.

The invasion of the Normans gave England strong links with France that would last for centuries to come. One of the most important influences the Normans would have in the north was in the establishment of great abbeys and monasteries. Frenchmen who belonged to monastic orders like the Cistercians often established these abbeys in Britain. They came to settle here at the invitation of the English or Scottish kings and barons. Some of these monastic sites have French names and include Jervaulx in Wensleydale and Rievaulx in Ryedale, both of which are in Yorkshire. Both names are French and take their name from their valley settings. Jervaulx means Ure valley, because the Ure is the river of Wensleydale, while Rievaulx means Rye Valley. A more surprising French name connected with a monastic site is the former mining town of Bearpark, a few miles to the west of Durham. This lies close to a medieval retreat used by the monks of Durham and is a corruption of the original French name Beau Repaire meaning 'Beautiful Retreat'.

Chester-le-Street, Thornton-le-Beans and Walton-le-Dale

A large number of place-names contain the Norman element 'le' in hyphenated form. The Normans used this to ensure accurate identification and was necessary for the purposes of taxation and other administration. It usually occurs in place-names that are found more than once. For example in County Durham, the territory of the Norman Prince Bishops we find places called Haughton-le-Skerne, Houghton-le-Spring, Hetton-le-Hole and Hetton-le-Hill. Each name was given a distinguishing feature so that it could be clearly identified. A name like Hetton-le-Hole can for example be interpreted to mean 'the Hetton in the Hollow'. Other examples of this kind of name include Thornton-le-Street in Yorkshire and Chester-le-Street in Durham, both named from their location on a Roman road. Also in Yorkshire are Thornton-le-Beans, Hutton-le-Hole and Adwick-le-Street. Examples in Lancashire and Cheshire include Walton-le-Dale and Whittle-le-Woods near Preston and Thornton-le-Moors near Chester. The place Hartlepool although it is not hyphenated came about in the same way. It is named to distinguish it from the nearby village of Hart and means Hart near the pool or bay.

Part Eight:
First Names and Family Names

nderson, Canute Barlow, (
)ixon, Oswulf Davidson, Al
son, William Guthfrithson,
mpson, Baldric Braithwai
sgrave, Snaebjorn Scott, H
licholson, Richard Hende
th, Osmund Nixon, Gospat
, Dutton, Bjarni Littlefair,
lson, Adam Thornton, Wil
Law, Godric Wells, Ralph tl
White, Siga Johnson, Edwa
at, Edmund Robson, Philij
ze Chapman, William Gra;
,seltine, Geoffrey Heron, Gi

Northern Names, Old and New

Part Eight:
First Names and Family Names

Norman Names in the Domesday Book

Norman place-names in Britain may be few and far between, but when it comes to personal names, the Normans changed our history forever. Normans introduced new Christian names to Britain that would gradually replace the old Anglo-Saxon and Viking names in popularity. The influence of these names is so great that today we tend to think of Norman-French names as being typically English. By contrast, we often look upon the older English and Viking names as being foreign, or at the least very old-fashioned. Because the names of English people before 1066 seem so strange to us today, it often makes the pre-conquest history of our country seem much more remote.

The Egberts, Oswulfs and Orms of our distant past are perceived by some as if they were myths from another world, while the Williams, Henrys and Richards of the later Medieval period are accepted more readily as part of our English history. There is a tendency to distant ourselves from the earlier Germanic and Scandinavian folk, despite the fact that they named most of the towns and counties in which we live and despite the fact that we can trace our local dialects and regional identity back to their time.

The Anglo-Saxon and Viking ages are just as much a part of our history as the Tudors and Stuarts or the Industrial Revolution.

Richard the Lionheart

Norman names like Richard seem more English than older Anglo-Saxon names like Egbert or Oswulf. This is deceptive. The Norman King of England, Richard I, known as 'Richard the Lionheart' has often been portrayed as a heroic English monarch. However, Richard couldn't speak English, he only knew French and hardly ever visited England.

Names in the Domesday Book

In the Domesday Book of 1086 we can see a written record of how changes were taking place by simply looking at the names of people. In the Yorkshire section of the Domesday Book many of the named people still seem to have names of Viking or Anglo-Saxon origin. However most of these people are the men who held various parcels of land before 1066. In many cases their lands had passed into the hands of a small number of Normans after 1066. That is not to say that the people with the Anglo-Saxon and Viking names were eliminated. It merely meant that a small number of Normans were now the major landholders in the north. Many people of Anglo-Saxon, Viking or Celtic ancestry would now find themselves working for the Normans as servants or workers with varying degrees of status.

The Domesday Book was not a complete census of every person in England but was primarily a record of those who held the land before 1066 and those who held it after that date. Most individuals like peasants would not warrant a mention. Nevertheless, almost 500 of the more influential members of Yorkshire society are mentioned in the Yorkshire section of the Domesday Book. Many of these have Anglo-Saxon or Viking names but the new Norman landholders are also listed with names like William, Hugh, Nigel, Gilbert, Geoffrey, Richard, Robert, Alan, Roger and Ralph. These Norman names seem unremarkable by modern standards and many are still very numerous today. By comparison, the Anglo-Saxon and Viking names listed in the book seem to belong to a very different age.

Old Names in the Yorkshire Domesday Book

The following Anglo-Saxon and Viking names are among those mentioned in the Yorkshire section of the Domesday Book:

Aegelfride, Aethelwulf, Aldwulf, Alfred, Almund, Alwine, Arnbjorn, Arngrimr, Arnketil, Arnthorr, Asmundr, Baldric, Bjarni, Bjornulfr, Bjorr, Brandulfr, Dolgfinnr, Eadmund, Eadric, Earnwine, Edwin, Egbrand, Eilafr, Esbjorn, Fargrimr, Finnghall, Gamalbarn, Gamalkarl, Gamall, Gilli, Godred, Godric, Godwin, Gospatric, Grimmr, Gunnarr, Halfdan, Harold, Ingjalar, Ketilbjorn, Knutr, Leofing, Leafsige, Ligulf, Maccus, Madalgrimm, Morcar, Muli, Northmann, Oddi, Ormr, Osbern, Siward, Skali, Snaebjorn, Snarri, Steinn, Sumarfugl, Sunnurfugl, Sunnulfr, Sveinn, Thorfinr, Thorfrothr, Thorketil, Thorr, Thorstein, Toki, Tosti, Uhtred, Ulfketil, Ulfr, Wicga.

Names in the Boldon Book

In 1183 'the Boldon Book', County Durham's equivalent of the Domesday Book was instigated by the Prince Bishop Hugh Du Puiset who is better known as Bishop Pudsey. As with the Yorkshire Domesday Book, Boldon Book shows a mixture of Norman, Anglo-Saxon and Viking personal names amongst the more influential population of the county.

The criteria of the Boldon Book was slightly different to that of the Domesday Book, so we should be cautious in making comparisons, but there appears to have been a higher proportion of Norman names in the Boldon Book. This is perhaps not altogether surprising since the Normans had ruled England for 117 years when the Boldon Book survey was carried out. The Normans had only been in power twenty years at the time of the Domesday Book.

Among the typical Norman names recorded in the Boldon Book are Hugh, Nigel, William, Richard, Robert, Gerard, Roger, Lawrence, Geoffrey, Ralph, Alan, Gilbert, Guy, Henry, John, Philip, Ranulph, Simon, Thomas and Walter. There is still a wide selection of people with the older English and Scandinavian names mentioned in the Boldon Book. Thus we have Godric, Toki, Aldred, Sigga, Edward, Osmund, Turkill, Gospatrick, Elwin, Lefwine, Edulf, Liulf, Thore, Uctred, Waldwin, Edmund, Anketill, Amfrid and Etheldred.

However, like the Domesday Book, Boldon Book concentrates on wealthy landholders. Perhaps Anglo-Saxon and Viking names were even more common amongst the peasantry. Of course, it is also important to note that having a Viking first name would not necessarily mean that the individual was of Viking descent, just as having an Anglo-Saxon or Norman name would not necessarily be proof of Anglo-Saxon or Norman descent. Indeed there was a good chance that Norman names would become fashionable amongst non-Normans wishing to emulate their powerful masters.

Nicknames and Surnames

An interesting feature of the names in the Boldon Book is that many of the people mentioned also have a descriptive name that explains exactly who they are. These are the kind of names that might eventually develop into surnames. Thus we have Adam the Clerk, Adam of Selaby, Adam the Reeve and Adam of Thornton. Then we have Alan the Fuller, Alan Son of Osbert, Alan the Cobbler, Alan of Chilton, Osbert son of Bosing, Osbert of Selaby, Osbert Rat, Aldred Boner, Aldred the Smith, Ralph the Crafty, Ralph the Clerk and Ralph Son of William.

Most of these names cannot be regarded as surnames because they apply specifically to the individual rather than a family name. In other words Adam the Clerk was actually a clerk by trade, while Osbert of Selaby was very probably from the place called Selaby. Most names of this type had not yet become fixed as surnames. Some surnames were developing at this period, but the establishment of fixed surnames tended to occur later in the 1200s and 1300s.

After 1066, many of the powerful barons in the North and Scotland would be of Norman descent. The surnames of powerful medieval barons like Percy, Neville, Mowbray, Balliol and Bruce were names of Norman French origin.

Many of these hereditary family names became fixed as surnames quite early in the Norman period and often derived from place-names in France.

Vikings didn't have surnames

Permanent surnames were very uncommon before the Norman Conquest. It is sometimes mistakenly thought that the Vikings had surnames but these were not proper surnames like we have today. Viking second names were not passed onto children in a fixed form. For example if a Viking by the name of Olaf had a son called Eric, this son would be called Eric Olafson because he was the son of Olaf. If Eric then had a son called Orm, this son would be called Orm Ericsson because he was the son of Eric and so on. This kind of naming practice survived in Scandinavian countries until recent centuries, but died in Britain at about the time of the Norman Conquest. The predominance in northern England of surnames ending in the word 'son' is sometimes thought to be of Scandinavian origin, but surname scholars have found little evidence that surnames of this type go back to Viking times. In fact surnames ending in 'son' seem to have developed at a later period.

It was in the centuries following the conquest that fixed surnames came to be more firmly established amongst the ordinary people. As the Normans increased the strength of their hold on Britain, and as population increased, the need to identify people for the purposes of administration became more important and surnames became necessary.

Surnames provide an important clue to the origins of people in the North, but since most surnames only developed after 1066 it is very difficult for most families to reliably trace their roots back to Anglo-Saxon or Viking times. Nevertheless surnames give us interesting clues to the movement of people in the last thousand years and an insight into the occupations, appearance or regional origin of some of our ancestors.

Types of Surnames

Surnames can provide a useful clue to the origins of the people of the North. Most surnames developed in the Middle Ages in the centuries that followed the Norman Conquest. In general terms, surnames fall into four broad categories:

1. Relationship surnames.

2. Location surnames.

3. Nickname surnames.

4. Occupational surnames.

Relationship surnames are quite common in the north and many simply end in the word 'son'. Names like these tell us the name of the father of the first person to use the surname. Relationship surnames closely associated with the North include Davidson, Dixon (Son of Richard), Gibson (Son of Gilbert) Hodgson (Son of Roger), Henderson (son of Henry), Nicholson, Nixon, Coulson (son of Nicholas) and Robinson (Son of Robin, Robert). Other names associated with the North include Robson, Stephenson, Wilson, Watson, Simpson (son of Simon) and Anderson (son of Andrew). Many of these names are also very numerous in Scotland.

Location surnames are often northern in origin and tell us where the first person to use the surname came from. Location names can also refer to features in the landscape. For example, the surname Law derives from an Anglo-Saxon word for hill that is commonly used in the north. The surname Myers comes from an Old Norse word for a marsh. People with such names had ancestors who lived on or near a hill or close to a marsh. It doesn't necessarily mean they have Anglo-Saxon or Viking ancestors.

Nickname Surnames can take many forms. For example the surname Heron, might refer to someone with long legs. Often these types of names are a colour like Black, or White or Brown, perhaps describing the colour of a person's hair or eyes. A tall person might be called Storey, whilst a short person may simply be called Little. A beefy person could be called Metcalfe (meaty calf) and a bald person might be called Ball. A strong person could be called Armstrong or Turnbull and a 'bonny' person might be called Bell (Belle).

Occupational surnames describe a person's employment and are more likely to have originated in the south than in the north. However some surnames like Walker meaning a 'cloth worker' seem to be most predominant in the north of England. The most familiar occupational surname is of course Smith (a farrier), which is widespread everywhere in the British Isles. Other familiar names of this kind include Taylor (a tailor), Clark or Clarke (a cleric) and Chapman (a trader). Occupational names closely associated with the north include Barker (a tanner) which is numerous in Yorkshire, Forster (a forester) and Jagger, an old name for a carter in Yorkshire.

Surnames and their origins

Anderson: Numerous in the north. The name derives from Andrew. Particularly numerous in Scotland where it was first recorded in the 1400s. Its predominance there is perhaps due to St Andrew being the patron saint. The name Anders is also a Scandinavian form of Andrew.

Atkinson: Son of Adkin. Numerous in the North and recorded in Westmorland in 1404.

Chapman: This name means trader or merchant and its first recorded occurrence was in Yorkshire in 1206. The name is likely to be older, since it is also recorded in Derbyshire in the following year and in the south of England in the 1300s. The name derives from an Anglo-Saxon word 'Ceapian' meaning to bargain, trade, barter or buy.

Davidson and Davison: Son of David. This surname is Numerous in the north. It occurs in Yorkshire as Davyson as early as 1350.

Forster and Foster: Foster probably refers to a person who was a foster parent or foster child. Forster means 'a forester or forest worker'. The name is quite closely associated with Northumberland and the Border region but probably originated in the south of England.

Gibson: Son of Gibbe, probably a shortened form of Gilbert. Occurs in Yorkshire as early as 1484.

Gray or Grey: Refers to a person with grey hair, grey eyes or perhaps a grey personality.

Hall: A person who lived or worked in a hall. The surname is widespread throughout Britain.

Harrison: Recorded in Yorkshire as early as 1445. In earlier times Henryson was probably used.

Henderson: Numerous in the north of England, but most likely of Scottish origin. It means son of Henry. It was recorded in Scotland as early as 1374.

Heron: A reference to a person with skinny legs or perhaps deriving from 'de Harum', or 'de Harome'. Harome was a place near Helmsley in North Yorkshire. Recorded in the Helmsey area of Yorkshire as Hairun in 1196.

Heseltine: A Yorkshire surname. Means the hazel dene - a valley with hazel trees. It occurs in Yorkshire as Haseldine in 1258 and in Durham as Hesledene in 1243.

Hodgson: Son of Hodge, a nickname for Roger. Occurs in Lancashire and Yorkshire as Hoggeson in 1381 and in Yorkshire as Hodgson in 1525.

Holmes: A person who originates from a water meadow or island. It derives from the Viking word 'Holmr'.

Hudson: Occurs as Hutson in Yorkshire in 1323. Means son of Hudde.

Hutchinson: Early forms of this name occur in Yorkshire as Huchonson 1379 and Hucheson in 1440.

Jamieson: The surname Jameson occurs in Yorkshire as early as 1379.

Lister: A surname that predominates in Yorkshire. Derives from Litster through the Scandinavian word Litt - to dye. A Lister was a cloth dyer. First recorded in Yorkshire as Litster in 1286

Nicholson: Son of Nicholas. This is a widespread surname in the north. Occured in Scotland as Nycholson in 1443

Patterson: Numerous in the north and particularly in Scotland. Also occurs as Pattison and Paterson. It means son of Patrick. Occurs in Scotland in 1446.

Richardson: Son of Richard. Occurs in Scotland as Richardesson in 1359 and as Richardson in 1381

Robinson: Son of Robin or Robert. Occurs in Yorkshire as Robynson in 1324. First recorded in Lancashire in 1332.

Robson: Son of Robert. First recorded in Yorkshire in 1379.

Simpson: The earliest recorded owner of the name was a Richard Symmeson of Staffordshire in 1353 and the first mention in the north was Adam Symson in Yorkshire in 1395. Simpson with the 'p' first occurs in 1397 when a John Simpson is recorded in Yorkshire. The P is a 'parasitic glide consonant', it simply crept into the names Symson and Simson through pronunciation.

Smith: A person who works with metal, usually a blacksmith. Common everywhere, in Scotland, England and Wales. One of the earliest recorded Smiths was an Ecceard Smith who lived in County Durham in 975 AD.

Sykes: A Yorkshire surname that derives from an old word for a boundary stream. The name has been the subject of considerable study. Professor Bryan Sykes, of the University of Oxford, an expert in genetic research believed that surnames are "written in your genes". The Professor undertook a DNA survey of 250 people around the country who shared his surname. He discovered that a distinctive gene was shared by most of the holders of this surname suggesting that all were descended from a single individual who lived in medieval times. His research proved that distinctive genes were also associated with other surnames. Of course some incidences of infidelity, or adoption over the centuries would mean that not all members of the Sykes family would share the distinctive gene.

Thompson: Occurs in Scotland as Thomson in 1318 and in Yorkshire as Thompson in 1349.

Walker: As a proportion of the population, the surname Walker is most numerous in the Teesside area and is also found in large numbers around Leeds and Wakefield. This does not mean that the surname originated in one of those areas but it is very likely to be northern in origin. The surname is first recorded in the north in Yorkshire in 1260 as 'Le Walker'. This was an occupational name. Walkers were involved in the cloth-making process. A Walker scoured and thickened raw cloth by beating it in water. Men who trampled or walked on the cloth in a trough originally performed this process. Hence the surname Walker.

Watson: Son of Wat or Watt, probably an old shortened form of Walter. The surname is numerous in Scotland and the north. Recorded in Yorkshire in 1324.

Wilson: Son of Will or William. Recorded in Yorkshire as Willeson in 1324 and as Wilson in 1341.

Surnames from Places

Many people in the north have surnames that derive from places in the north of England. For example the surname Ackroyd comes from a place called Ackroyd in Yorkshire. The place-name means 'oak road', but the surname means 'person from Ackroyd'. (see right)

Ackroyd: (Yorkshire); **Applegarth**: (Yorkshire and Cumbria); **Appleton**: (Yorkshire); **Appleyard**: (Yorkshire); **Askew**: (Yorkshire); **Asquith**: (from Askwith in Yorkshire).

Bainbridge: (Yorkshire); **Barlow**: (Lancashire); **Blackburn**: (Yorkshire or Scotland); **Blenkinsopp**: (Northumberland); **Bolam**: (Northumberland or Durham.); **Bowes**: (Yorkshire); **Braithwaite**: (either Yorkshire or Cumbria); **Bruce**: (from a place in France); **Burdon**: (County Durham).

Carr: (from a marshy area, probably in the North); **Copeland**: (Cumbria); **Coverdale**: (Yorkshire); **Crosby**: (Cumbria or Lancashire).

Dewhurst: (Lancashire.); **Dinsdale**: (Durham); **Duckworth**: (Lancashire); **Dutton**: (Lancashire or Cheshire).

Featherstonehaugh: (Northumberland.); **Fenwick**: (Yorkshire or Northumberland).

Gascgoine: from the Gascony region of France.); **Grimshaw**: (Lancashire).

Hall: (from a hall, probably in the North); **Harbottle**: (Northumberland); **Hardcastle**: (Yorkshire); **Hardwick**: (from a place called Hardwick of which there are several); **Hepburn**: (Northumberland); **Heppell**: (Northumberland); **Hollingsworth**: (Cheshire or Lancashire).

Jarvis: (from Jervaulx in Yorkshire).

Kellett: (Yorkshire in Lancashire or Cumbria); **Kerr**: from a place near a marshy or poor quality area of land.); **Kershaw**: (Lancashire).

Lambton: (Durham); **Liddell**: (from Liddesdale in Scotland); **Lumley**: (Durham).

Mowbray: (France); **Murray**: (from the Moray region of Scotland); **Musgrave**: (Cumbria).

Neville: (France).

Ord: (Northumberland).

Pendlebury: (Lancashire); **Percy**: (France); **Pickering**: (Yorkshire); **Pickersgill**: (Yorkshire).

Ramsbottom: (Lancashire).

Scott: (a person from Scotland); **Shafto**: (Northumberland.); **Strickland**: (Cumbria); **Surtees**: (from a place on the River Tees).

Thirlwall: (Northumberland on Hadrian's Wall).

Washington: (Durham); **Welsh**: (a person from Wales).

Part Nine:
Scots and Border Folk

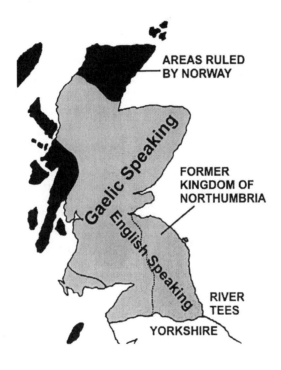

AREAS RULED
BY NORWAY

Gaelic Speaking

English Speaking

FORMER
KINGDOM OF
NORTHUMBRIA

RIVER
TEES

YORKSHIRE

Scotland and the North Circa 1142

Part Nine:
Scots and Border Folk

Scots in Northern England

As might be expected many people in the North of England are descended from Scots. Scottish influence in northern England has a long history and many people in the North of England have surnames that can be instantly identified as Scottish, even though some of these families may have lived in England for centuries. Look at any northern English telephone directory and you will discover that there are thousands upon thousands of northerners with Scottish surnames.

Scots have long been present in England's population and not just in the north. In the Subsidy Rolls for Suffolk in 1327, 35 people were recorded with the surname Skot. It is thought they were descended from retainers of King David of Scotland, who held land in eastern England. Alternatively they could have been Scots who had supported King Edward I against Robert the Bruce. If so, these people had acquired surnames that identified their nationality as 'Scottish'. However another theory is that the name was connected with a French word Escoute meaning 'spy'. If they were Scottish this would not have been inappropriate since many Scots in England at that time were eyed with suspicion and often accused of being spies.

Thousands of Scots came to live in England both permanently and temporarily during the Middle Ages even though many suffered hostility during political tensions between England and Scotland. Tension was increased by the long-running alliance between Scotland and France which made the English paranoid. In 1440, as a result of the French wars, taxes called 'alien subsidies' were introduced. This, along with a later commission set up in 1543 to identify all Scots in English counties, suggests that there were a substantial number of Scots living in England at the time. It was especially the case in the far northern counties of Cumberland and Westmorland where many Scots lived as householders or servants.

Scottish Surnames

Typical Scottish clan names from the highland region of Scotland often begin with the Gaelic word Mac meaning 'son of'. Thus we have names like MacDonald, MacDougal, MacKenzie, MacGregor and many others. By contrast clan names from the eastern coast of Scotland as far north as Aberdeen have names that look less typically Gaelic. These names often appear to be English, Scandinavian or Norman in origin. Clan names from this eastern area of Scotland include Carnegie, Gordon, Burnett, Leslie, Hay, Keith, Baird, Cumming and Forbes. In the far north we find the original homeland of the clan name Gunn. This is a name of Scandinavian origin and demonstrates the Norwegian influence that once existed in this region.

After Culloden

Most early movement of Scots probably involved lowlanders, but there was significant population movement of Highland Scots after the Battle of Culloden in 1746. The battle brought an end to the Jacobite rebellions and set in motion the destruction of the highland clan society. In the highlands of Scotland people had grouped themselves into clans and lived as farmers often by means of raiding and rustling each other's livestock. The Scottish Clans had their own rights of jurisdiction and their own courts, independent of the king's law. Like kings, clan leaders could command military service from men who were often loyal to the clan above the nation. Clan chiefs could muster forces of up to 3,000 men. People often allied themselves to particular clans and adopted the clan name for themselves and their children regardless of their original surname. For example someone called Smith might ally himself to the McDougal clan and adopt the McDougal name for himself and his family. This meant that over time, the names of particularly powerful clans like MacDonald or McKenzie would become increasingly common surnames and indeed such surnames are extremely numerous today.

After 1746 the clan system was gradually destroyed and depopulation of the highland region followed. Over time clansmen found their way into lowland areas, many finding their way into Glasgow, or into the Scottish lowlands and many settled much further afield in Australia or America. A large number settled in Canada. A significant outpouring of highland Scots into other areas occurred in the early nineteenth century stimulated by an agricultural famine and the promise of work in the expanding industrial areas. Over the decades many people who could trace their origin back to the Scottish highlands found their way into England including the industrial towns and cities of the north.

Many Lowland Scots would also head for England over a considerable period of time. Many were attracted by the textile industries of Yorkshire and Lancashire, since the making of textiles was a well-established industry in the Scottish lowlands. Northern towns may have offered new opportunities and a chance to develop a career.

Border Surnames

Surnames originating from the Scottish Border region never begin with the Gaelic word 'Mac', because southern Scotland was not a Gaelic-speaking region. The surnames originating from the southern and border regions are virtually indistinguishable from those on the English side and its often difficult to know where they actually originated.

Typical names originating or most commonly found in the border region include names like Armstrong, Charlton, Milburn, Robson, Dodd, Hetherington, Heron, Maxwell, Hume, Graham, Home, Turnbull, Johnston, Nixon, Dixon, Selby, Hall, Carr, Ker, Ridley, Elliott, Trotter and Fenwick. Often these were clan names belonging to the Border Reivers, a society of raiding clans or 'Graynes' found in both England and Scotland. The Border Reivers were a particularly distinct group whose focus lay on both side of the Anglo-Scottish divide. The history of these people should be regarded as quite distinct from that of the traditional Gaelic clans of the Scottish highlands.

The Normans in Scotland

The centuries of conflict that have characterised the historical relationship between Scotland and northern England often overshadow the strong cultural links that once existed between the two. Political boundaries have served to emphasise the differences between the people of the two nations but it seems that in earlier times the people of Scotland and northern England were even more closely related than they are today.

When the Normans conquered England their conquest of at least part of Scotland would inevitably follow. Scottish kings like Alexander I and his brother David I avoided the expected Norman military invasion of their country by encouraging powerful Norman families to settle in the land north of the Border. These Scottish Normans became part of the aristocracy and gradually introduced castle building and Feudalism to Scotland. Many of the most powerful figures in Scottish history after 1066 were Normans. Families of Norman origin in Scotland include the Bruces and Baliols, both of which produced Kings of Scotland.

Norman influence in Scotland gained much ground during the reign of King David I of Scotland (1124-1153). David had been brought up in England under strong Anglo-Norman influence and this made a lasting impression upon his life. David played a major part in encouraging Norman cultural influences in Scotland.

David forged a close alliance with Thurstan, the Archbishop of York who was one of the most powerful Norman figures in the North of England. Through this influence David established a number of Norman-French monasteries north of the border. Many of these monasteries had strong links with monasteries in both Yorkshire and France. French, Scottish or Yorkshire monks from continental orders like the Cistercians would come to settle in Scotland.

Robert the Bruce of Hartlepool

The Scottish name Bruce was originally a Norman name originating in France. The name was originally De Brus and derives from Briouze in France. The De Bruses came to Britain in Norman times and settled in the Hartlepool and Guisborough areas to the north and south of the River Tees. They helped to defend England against the Scots at the Battle of the Standard near Northallerton in 1138. However, the family also held land in Annandale in Scotland and they gradually came to focus their attentions there. The most famous Bruce was of course Robert the Bruce the King of Scotland (1274-1329).

Northumberland and Scotland – the Common Cultural Links

Melrose on the banks of the River Tweed was among the monasteries founded by King David in Scotland. An earlier monastery had existed here in the days when Melrose had been part of the Kingdom of Northumbria. Melrose was a monastery that had been associated with the famed Northumbrian saint, Cuthbert, who was born nearby and its establishment may have rekindled the strong cultural and historical links between lowland Scotland and the North of England.

King David came to be involved in an English political dispute that would draw further attention to the cultural links between Scotland and the North. His actions brought the political and cultural future of at least one part of Northern England into question.

David recognised the historic links between lowland Scotland and northern England that went back to the days when the Scottish lowlands had been part of Northumbria. In terms of language and cultural heritage, the Scottish lowlands were much closer to Northern England than they were to the Gaelic speaking Highlands or to the Norwegian speaking Shetlands and Orkneys of the time. The Islands, along with Caithness in the far north of Scotland and Argyll in the west, still belonged to the Kingdom of Norway.

In David's time, it is likely that there was already a well established 'Border identity' shared between Northumberland, Cumberland and the lowlands of Scotland that went back to the days of the Northumbrian kingdom. Although this cultural link was often strained by tensions between the two nations, it would last for several centuries to come. The link was perhaps strongest in terms of language with northern English having much more in common with Scotland than the dialects of the south.

Scottish claims to the North

David's kingdom of Scotland was focused on the Scottish lowlands and indeed his kingdom stretched into Cumberland, a region that had been under Scottish rule since 1135. In fact David often resided at Carlisle and this was in effect the capital city of Scotland during his reign. However, the eastern lowlands of Scotland were at the very heart of David's kingdom. This was a region historically known as Lothian that had once extended as far south as the Tweed.

The Lothians had only ceased to be part of Northumbria in 1018 when the Scots had seized the land from the Northumbrians and extended their nation's boundaries to the banks of the Tweed. Even Edinburgh had been part of Northumbria until as recently as 954. Neither Edinburgh nor the lowlands had been part of Scotland in earlier times. In fact before the days of Northumbria they had belonged to a Welsh speaking tribe called the Gododdin. The links between Northumbria and the Scottish lowlands would still have been fresh in many minds during David's reign.

David's marriage to the granddaughter of Siward, the late Earl of Northumbria, made David even more acutely aware of the links between Scotland and Northumbria. Siward had played an important part in shaping Scottish history, including a major part in the defeat of the Scottish King Macbeth. He also played a big part in the appointment of Macbeth's successor, Malcolm III.

King David's marriage to a descendant of Siward meant that his son Henry had a hereditary claim to the Earldom of Northumbria. All of these factors gave David a very strong incentive for bringing at least one part of Northern England under his family's Scottish control.

North East England was once part of Scotland

King David I may have looked for opportunities to extend his influence southward into Northumberland. The opportunity came in 1135, when a war arose between Stephen, the King of England, and Matilda, daughter of the late Henry I. David sided with Matilda, after Stephen denied David's family claims in Northumberland. David used the dispute between Stephen and Matilda as an excuse for invading England in 1138. He gained some support from Norman barons on both sides of the Border but his invasion was not initially a success. He was defeated at the Battle of the Standard near Northallerton and his old ally Archbishop Thurstan of York fought against him.

The battle did not, however, bring an end to David's Northumbrian claims. A peace treaty was signed at Durham the following year in which David's son Henry was given Northumberland. To all intents and purposes Northumberland, which at that time included land along the northern bank of the Tees, came under Scottish control. In 1141 David made further territorial gains when his Chancellor, William Cumin, succeeded in seizing the County Palatine of Durham from the Prince Bishops. This brought the whole of North East England under virtual Scottish control.

However this situation was not to last. The North East and Cumberland were reclaimed from Scotland by Stephen's powerful successor, Henry II in 1157. If Henry had not reclaimed this land then the Scottish border would surely have followed the course of the River Tees even to this day. The North Eastern part of England would have developed a very different history, culture and language as a part of Scotland. Other parts of northern England would also have seen an effect. The Scottish culture and language might have developed differently if the focus of the nation had stretched so much further south. Of course this is only speculation and it is impossible to know what would have really happened if history had taken a different course.

Scottish claims in the North East

The northern part of the Kingdom of Northumbria called Bernicia originally extended from the Tees to the Firth of Forth and had long attracted Scottish interest. In 974 AD Edgar the King of England met with Kenneth the King of the Scots and several other kings at Chester in the North West. The future of Bernicia is thought to have been on the agenda, but Edgar made it clear that Bernicia belonged to England. However the Scots continued to raid and eventually seized the northern half of Bernicia as far south as the River Tweed in the year 1018. There always remained a possibility that Scotland's boundaries could be extended further, but this only became a reality in the period 1139 to 1157 during the reign of King David.

The far northern English regions of Northumberland, Durham and Cumberland were returned to England and English they remained. Border disputes and raiding would effect the whole region in the centuries to come and shape the lives and culture of the people. Raiding and dispute were a constant cultural feature of these far northern counties until the 1600s. Ironically this troublesome way of life unified the whole border region with a common cultural identity and perhaps these strong cultural links still exist to this day albeit on more peaceful terms.

Scottish Tynedale

Even after 1157 the Scots were allowed to keep certain rights in the Tynedale region of Northumberland and the Scottish kings consistently made claims of sovereignty in Tynedale. On one occasion in 1314, the people of Tynedale proclaimed Robert the Bruce their King. For centuries Tynedale would be one of the most troublesome parts of the border and was a hot bed of Border reiving activity. Tynedale had been granted a special liberty status by the Normans so that it could be administered as an important defended region on the Border. Henry VIII abolished the liberty in 1495 and the region increasingly became lawless. Thomas Wolsey closed all the churches in Tynedale as a result of the "evil irregularities" of its priests.

The Troublesome Border

When Henry II reclaimed Northumberland and Cumberland from the Scots in 1157 it did not bring an end to the Border troubles. For centuries raiding continuously troubled the whole border region.

Northumberland and neighbouring counties on both sides of the border were caught up in the England-Scotland struggle. Monarchs on the English and the Scottish side often encouraged the raids. Encouraging trouble in the Border regions served as a means of deterring full-scale attack in either direction.

The Border country was like a football that was kicked by both sides. Thus the years of war and raiding brought anarchy and chaos to the whole region.

Furthermore, the borders were severely overcrowded in those days. Land was often divided up by fathers amongst their sons in a practice rooted in Anglo-Saxon times.

This resulted in there being barely enough land to sustain each family. Families could only recover from devastating raids by forming huge clan groups that regarded the theft of cattle, sheep, goats, pigs and household goods from rival clans as the only way to live. All of this helped in the creation of a distinct Border culture based on a life of raiding and revenge.

The Border Reivers

Many of the people on both sides of the Border were 'Border Reivers', who regarded allegiance to a family clan as far more important than nationality. The Border folk, both English and Scottish, shared a common culture, a similar dialect and a deep-rooted history. They cared little for allegiance to a particular crown, whether it was Scottish or English. In many cases clan groups straddled both sides of the border.

Reivers were especially active in Tudor times when Henry VIII encouraged raiding. The reiver lifestyle was characterised by raiding, livestock rustling and blood feud between family groups. Their behaviour seemed like a throwback to the days of the warlike Britons, Vikings or Anglo-Saxons from whom many of the reivers were probably descended. Indeed, like the warriors of old, they enjoyed nothing more than composing ballads that glorified raiding and revenge.

The nineneenth century historian G.M. Tevelyan described the Border Reivers as:

"Cruel, coarse savages, slaying each other like the beasts of the forest; and yet they were also poets who could express in the grand style the inexorable fate of the individual man and woman, the infinite pity for all cruel things which they none the less inflicted upon one another. It was not one ballad-maker alone but the whole cut throat population who felt this magnanimous sorrow, and the consoling charms of the highest poetry."

Some Reivers lived in fortified tower houses called Bastles and Peles but most lived in primitive clay houses that could be rebuilt in a day, as they were often destroyed in Border raiding.

Like many Northerners today, the Reivers enjoyed a good game of football although these could often end in violence. Some of these games lasted from dusk to dawn and were especially popular amongst the Armstrong clan. It is a remarkable fact that many famous footballers of recent times often have reiver names like Milburn, Robson and Charlton.

Reiving ended when James I became King of both England and Scotland in 1603. Many of the most troublesome members of the reiver families like the Armstrongs were transported to Ireland. Today many surnames in Ireland can be traced back to the days of Border Reiving.

Red-Handed Black Mail

Reivers invented phrases like 'Red-Handed' and 'Blackmail'. Red Hand refers to raiders caught stealing livestock that was coloured with red dye for identification. Reivers who were caught red-handed were often hanged on the spot. Black Mail or Black Rent was a 'Protection Racket' or fee paid by tenant farmers to a chief Border Reiver in return for protection against raids.

The Lawless Clans

In the days of Border Reiving, feuds were often fought and raids were made, not in the name of England or Scotland, but in the name of a family like Armstrong or Robson. It was not an uncommon occurrence for English families to side with Scottish families in border feuds, especially as some of the Reiver surnames, like Armstrong, Hall and Graham were to be found on both sides of the border. This is an important consideration to make for people who can trace their family origins to the borders. Some family historians might for example assert that they are of Scottish descent when their family ancestors may in fact have been English Border Reivers.

Many of the families in the Border region had long running feuds during the age of border raiding. Blood feud was an ancient practice that could be traced back to the days of the Anglo-Saxons. However the particularly brutal form of feud practised by the reivers might go back to the earlier Celtic period.

The pattern of family feuds was often complicated. For example the Armstrongs on the Scottish side of the border had feuds with the Bells, Robsons, Musgraves and Ridleys on the English side as well as with the Turnbulls and Johnstones on the Scottish side.

The Armstrongs

The Armstrongs were one of the most famous Border Reiving clans. They included some of the most notorious Border Reivers like Kinmont Willie and Jock O' the Side. One theory traces their origins back to Siward Beorn, the son (or bairn) of Siward, the Anglo-Viking Earl of Northumbria. However it is also claimed that the Armstrongs were descended from a man called Fairbairn who was the armour bearer to the king of Scotland. There is a legend that Fairbairn lifted the king to safety from his dying horse, using only one arm, during a battle.

From that day on Fairbairn and his descendants were known as Armstrong. In the later centuries of Border Reiving many Armstrongs moved from Scotland into Cumberland. Some of the most powerful members of the Armstrong clan could call on the services of hundreds of men. The Armstrong surname is still particularly numerous in Northumberland, Cumbria and Durham today, but it is also found throughout the English speaking world. Undoubtedly the most famous descendant of this Border Reiving clan was a certain Neil Armstrong - the first man on the moon.

The brutality of the reivers is demonstrated by the well-known story that the Robsons of North Tynedale once made a foray into the Scottish valley of Liddesdale and stole a large flock of sheep belonging to the Graham family, which they brought back into Northumberland. Later it was discovered that the Graham sheep were infected with scab, which spread like wild fire through the Robson's flock.

The Robsons were so angry that they returned to Liddesdale in another raid, where they caught seven members of the Graham family and hanged them. They left a note to the effect that:

"The neist time gentlemen cam to tak their schepe. They are no te' be scabbit!"

Black Middens Bastle House, North Tynedale, a typical farmhouse of the Border Reiving age.

Border Reivers and their way of life, were certainly feared by outsiders and the Border Country had a certain element of mystique and danger about it. Even in the nearby walled town of Newcastle-upon-Tyne, there were rules forbidding the apprenticeship of men from the border valleys of North Tynedale and Redesdale to certain Newcastle trades, for fear that there might be trouble.

Fears may well have been justified for one Newcastle man writing of the Tynedale and Redesdale folk in 1649 records that:

"They come down from their dales into the low countries and carry away horses and cattle so cunningly that it will be hard for any to get them or their cattle except that they be aquainted with some master thief, who for safety money may help them to their stolen goods, or decieve them."

Elsdon Pele Tower, Redesdale, a typical fortified house of the Border Reiving age.

The Union of the Crowns in 1603 had largely brought an end to Border Reiving activity, though 'mosstroopers' and horse thieves were still active in the borders throughout the seventeenth century. It did not help that the very men who were supposed to be keeping the Border Reivers under control sometimes supported thieving activities. Indeed as late as 1701 a horse thief confessed that:

"The county keeper of Tynedale provided that they did not plunder his territory would connive at their stealing what they pleased in Scotland and in the adjacent Bishopric of Durham and would prosecute no one save those who stole from his own district".

When stability, law and order were brought to the Border region after the accession of James I to the throne in 1603, the activities of the Border Reivers gradually came to an end. Many of their descendants became keelmen on Tyneside, or Northumberland or Durham pitmen. Some of course moved

to new parts of Britain while others emigrated to Australia and the United States.

Border Reiver Surnames

The Border Reivers Circa 1500.

Bell: This is a common surname in Northumberland, Durham, Yorkshire and Scotland and included a clan of Border Reivers. The name could be a pet form of Isabel as was probably the case of Osbertus filius Bell who lived in Yorkshire in 1297. Alternatively the name could also refer to a bell-ringer, as was possibly the case of another Yorkshireman called Serlo Belle who lived in 1190. However, the exact origin of the border reiver Bells is not known.

Carr : Carr is a Border Reiver surname that also occurs in the form Carr, Kerr, Ker and Carre. The name derives from a Viking word 'Kjarr', meaning marshy or rough boggy country. The surname is commonest in Scotland and the north of England. The Border Reiving Carrs lived in fortified houses called pele towers. These were impregnable tower houses with walls three to four feet thick. Most had narrow spiral staircases, that ran upwards in a clockwise direction. It gave an advantage to right handed swordsmen defending their peles. The Carrs were different, as they were noted for being left handed, so their stairs ran in an anti-clockwise direction.

Charlton: Charlton, is a Border Reiving surname that derives from the Anglo-Saxon place-name Charlton. It means the farm belonging to a freed peasant or churl. Northumberland's reiving Charltons were associated with the Bellingham area of North Tynedale where there is a place called Charlton. Charltons were arch-enemies of the Scott family of Buccleugh in Hawick, Scotland.

Hesleyside Hall in North Tynedale was long associated with the Charltons. It was a tradition for the Lady of this house to bring a salver and dish for her hungry family at meal times. If the salver was lifted to reveal a riding spur, it was a signal that the larder was empty and that if they wanted food they would have to go raiding.

Dodd: The surname Dodd is primarily associated with Northumberland where the Dodds were one of the four major Border clans of North Tynedale. The others were the Milburns, Robsons and Charltons. Burbank Peel, a fortified tower on the Tarret Burn near Bellingham was the Dodds' ancestral home. Dodds are said to be descendeed from Eilaf, an Anglo-Saxon monk who was one of the carriers of St Cuthbert's coffin who fled from Lindisfarne at the time of the Viking raids in the 9th century. It is said that Eilaf pinched some cheese from his fellow monks who prayed that the culprit should be revealed by turning him into a Dodd -

an old word for a fox. According to the legend their prayers were answered and for a short while Eilaf was turned into a fox. From that day on Eilaf and his descendents were known as Dodd.

Eliott: This is a Border Reiver name very common in the North of England. The surname may derive from an Anglo-Saxon forename Elewald which means 'the elf ruler', or possibly from the name Elias. Heliot is an early form of the name recorded in Norman times. An Elliot was recorded in Somerset in the south of England in 1327 so the name may not necessarily have a northern origin, even though it is most numerous in the North. Until the 15th century the Elliott surname occurred in the Scottish Borders in the forms Elwald or Elwold. Spellings were often inconsistent and the name also occurred as Elwuad, Elwat, Elwood, Eluat, Eluott, Elioat and Elwand. Today there are at least seventy derivatives of the surname including four different spellings of the basic name - Eliot, Eliott, and Elliott. The last spelling was 'disowned' in the Scottish border according to an old rhyme:

The double L and single T descend from Minto and Wolflee,
the double T and single L mark the old race in Stobs that dwell,
The single L and single T the Eliots of St Germains be,
but double T and double L, who they are nobody can tell.

Fenwick: Robert de Ffenwick is the first recorded owner of the surname Fenwick and lived in the Scottish borders around 1220 but Fenwicks are also recorded in Lincolnshire in 1275 and a Thomas de Fenwyck is mentioned in Northumberland in 1279. The surname could derive from one of several places called Fenwick. The

Fenwicks were especially numerous in Northumberland and are still quite common in the North East region today.

Graham: The Grahams were notorious Border Reivers found on both sides of the Border. In 1552 the border Grahams were said to number five hundred and occupied thirteen fortified towers. One story claims that the Grahams were descended from a man called Graeme, who in Roman times is said to have helped to breach the Antonine Wall, a great wall between the Rivers Clyde and Forth. However this seems very unlikely. It is more likely that the Grahams were of Norman French origin and settled in the south of England at Grantham in Lincolnshire from which they took their name. The name De Grantham was corrupted to De Graham and later shortened to Graham. The Grahams moved to Scotland in the twelfth century, where a William De Graham is recorded in 1127.

Robson: Robson is very closely associated with Northumberland and Durham and was a common name amongst the coal miners of those two counties. It was also historically a Northumbrian 'Grayne' or family tribe of Border Reivers that inhabited the valley of North Tynedale in the Tudor period. One theory traces the family's origin to Hroethbert, an Anglo-Saxon mentioned on a runic cross that was found in North Tynedale.

Shafto: The Shaftos were a Northumbrian Border Reiving family who took their name from Shafto Crags near Morpeth. In later centuries their family members included a certain Robert Shafto who was an MP for County Durham. He was immortalised in the famous song Bonny Bobby Shafto.

Turnbull: In Scotland, the Border Reiving surname Turnbull occurred in early times as Turnebule and Tornebole both of which were recorded in the fourteenth century. It is a northern name long found on both sides of the border. Enemies of the Turnbulls included the Armstrong clan. Turnbull is a nickname and literally means 'turns bull' referring to a person's ability to become strong or brave when the need arose. Alternatively some have suggested the name derives from the French word 'Tourneboef' which means a drover. The surnames Trumble and Trimble are thought to be historical misspellings of the name Turnbull.

Coal Reivers and Keelmen

The Coal miners and 'Keelmen' of the industrial North East England were often descendants of the Border Reiver clans. This is why names like Robson, Charlton and Elliot are so common in the region today. In the 1600s Keelmen lived on the Newcastle Quayside in a street called Sandgate, outside Newcastle's walls. Keelmen were boatmen, who moved coal from the riverside to collier ships. The Keelmen took their name from small boats called Keels and were first recorded on the Tyne in the early 1300's. Like the Reivers, Keelmen were keen balladeers and their famous song the Keel Row is thought to have developed from an ancient Border ditty.

As aa cam' thro' Sandgate,
Thro' Sandgate, thro' Sandgate,
As aa cam' thro' Sandgate'
Aa heard a lassie sing:

Weel may the keel row,
The keel row, the keel row
Weel may the keel row
That ma laddie's in.

Border Reiver Surnames

ARMSTRONG	BEATTIE
BELL	BURN
CARLETON	CARLISLE
CARNABY	CARRUTHERS
CHAMBERLAIN	CHARLTON
COLLINGWOOD	CROZIER
CUTHBERT	DACRE
DAVISON	DIXON
DOUGLAS	DUNNE
ELLIOT	FENWICK
FORSTER	GRAHAM
GRAY	HALL
HENDERSON	HERON
HETHERINGTON	HODGSON
HUME	HUNTLEY
HUNTER	IRVING
JOHNSTONE	KERR
LAIDLAW	LITTLE
MAXWELL	MILBURN
NOBLE	OGLE
OLIVER	POTTS
PRINGLE	RADCLIFFE
RIDLEY	ROBSON
ROUTLEDGE	RUTHERFORD
SALKELD	SCOTT
SELBY	SHAFTOE
SIMPSON	STOREY
TAIT	THOMPSON
TURNBULL	WAKE
WATSON	WOODRINGTON
YARROW	YOUNG

Part Ten:
The Urban Age

A Victorian view of Newcastle

Part Ten:
The Urban Age

Northern England during the second millennium

The early sections of this book concentrated on the first millennium. In these chapters we found that a succession of invasions from overseas largely determined the origin of people in the North. Romans, Anglo-Saxons and Vikings were all invaders who brought major cultural and linguistic changes to the North.

For centuries, the descendants of these people lived in mostly rural settlements, scattered throughout the North. The legacy of each of these groups of people can still be found today. At the beginning of the second millennium, there was still one major invasion to come - the Norman invasion of 1066. The Normans also brought lasting cultural and linguistic changes to the North and were the only really significant influx of people up until the 1800s.

Towns, rather than villages began to emerge in the period from 1100 to 1400 when several places were granted town charters for the first time. The Towns first receiving charters during this period include Sunderland (1179), Gateshead (1179) and Preston (1179), Lancaster (1193), Liverpool (1207) and Manchester (1301). King Edward I established the port of Hull in 1293 and the port of Hartlepool was granted royal status in 1201. Newcastle also emerged as a major port during this period although in 1286 it was famed for the shipping of leather rather than coal. By 1305 Newcastle was regularly shipping coal to London.

The emergence of these towns in the medieval period was the earliest development of urbanisation in the north, but the towns were small by the standards of today. The only major town in Northern England throughout the medieval period was York, which had a population of around 10,000. Remarkably 10,000 is about the same as the estimated population of the entire county of Lancashire at the time of the Domesday Book.

On the whole, the movements of population during this period were relatively small. There would be no major invasion or settlement of people to bring about sudden and dramatic cultural changes like those that had occurred in the past. The only invaders were the Scots who raided the north on many occasions reaching as far south as the northern parts of Yorkshire and Lancashire. However, the Scots were usually invaders rather than settlers.

Of course there would have been some movement of people from Scotland and other regions into the north, but it is unlikely that there was any major change in the make up of the population as there had been during the Viking or Anglo-Saxon invasion.

The Population "Top of the Pops" 1334 - 1861

In his book 'Local History in England' W.G Hoskins compiled league tables of the forty-two most populous towns in England in the years 1334, 1377, 1527, 1662, 1801 and 1861. He used statistics compiled from tax quotas, poll tax returns and census figures. London was the most populous town throughout this period and was not included in the tables.

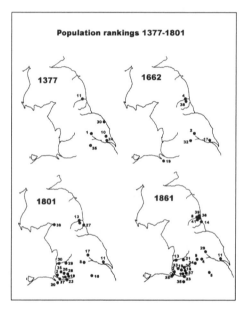

Population rankings 1377 – 1801: Numbers show population rankings in each year. For example, York is marked by the number 1 in 1377 because it was the most populous town in England after London.

Five of the medieval towns in the league table for 1334 were in the north of England. York ranked second after Bristol and Newcastle ranked third. The other northern towns to feature in the 1334 list were Beverley (15th), Hull (26th) and Scarborough (27th).

York had risen to first place by 1377 with Newcastle falling to 11th, just behind Beverley. Hull and Scarborough also featured in this table with the only other northern town being Pontefract in 35th place.

The Shambles, a medieval street in York. York was the most populous town in the North in medieval times.

In the 1520s the three most populous northern towns were Newcastle ranked 3rd, York ranked 14th and Hull ranked 21st. These three towns remained the most populous in the north in 1662, with York leaping ahead of Newcastle into second place behind Norwich. The only other northern towns to feature in the 1662 table are Chester (19th), Leeds (32nd) and Gateshead (38th).

Things had changed dramatically by the nineteenth century with eighteen northern towns featuring in the most populated list. In 1801 thirteen northern towns appear in the table for the first time. Astonishingly, Manchester and Liverpool were ranked first and second, even though they had not featured in the earlier tables. Another eight of the most populous towns were in the North West - namely Ashton under Lyne, Stockport, Bolton, Oldham, Blackburn, Preston, Wigan and Warrington. The only other northern towns to appear for the first time in the most populous list were Sheffield, Sunderland and Carlisle.

By 1861, twenty-three northern towns feature in Hoskins' 42 town league table with Liverpool and Manchester still at the top. Leeds (4th); Sheffield (5th); and Newcastle (8th) are also in the most populated list. Bradford makes its first appearance in the table in 9th position while Hull was 10th.

Newcastle is the only northern town to consistently appear in the top twenty of all the tables compiled by Hoskins. In fact it features in the top ten of each of the tables except for 1377 when it was 11th and in 1801 when it was ranked thirteenth.

Surname distribution and Traveling distances

The geographical distribution of surnames in historic times is one useful clue to the movement of people in the medieval period and later. Particular surnames were usually concentrated in specific localities, suggesting that family descendants rarely moved far from their place of origin. This makes it likely that many people in the pre-industrial north were in fact descended from the people who inhabited the region in Norman, Viking or Anglo-Saxon times.

As late as the eighteenth century most migration within Britain was of a very local nature, since marriage partners were rarely chosen from more than 10 miles away. Even where towns had started to grow, they generally attracted people from neighbouring rural areas. This was the case in industrial regions like the textile towns of Lancashire and Yorkshire, although particularly skilled workers in fields like iron working might travel much further.

Things would change considerably as the Industrial Revolution gained momentum in the 1700s and 1800s. The movement of people between regions increased and the population of the northern counties rose to astonishing levels that were previously unknown. Many families strayed further and further from their places of origin, particularly with the development of rail passenger transport that followed the opening of the Stockton and Darlington Railway and the Liverpool and Manchester Railway in the early 1800s. However, even in the 1800s there was still a great majority of northern people that strayed no further than the counties, towns or villages of their birth.

Textile Towns of Lancashire and Yorkshire

Significant cultural changes occurred in the population of the north during the eighteenth and nineteenth centuries. During this period, the total population of the north changed from being mostly rural to urban. Indeed the growth of industrial towns caused the population of Britain to more than double in the first half of the nineteenth century. The effects of this were felt no more so than in the North of England.

The invention of the steam engine, along with improvements in machinery such as the Hargreaves' Spinning Jenny of 1765 and Compton's Spinning Mule of 1779 coupled with the development of railways, enabled manufacturing to be carried out on a larger scale than ever known before. It shifted the economic and political balance of power away from the rural landowners towards the industrial capitalists. Furthermore the expanding British Empire created wealth that stimulated the growth of British towns.

The development of huge factories employing thousands of people encouraged massive increases of population in the north, accompanied by huge movements of population. Thousands upon thousands of people, many of who were previously agricultural workers left the land to find work in neighbouring towns. Many arrived in the north of England from other English counties in the midlands or the south while others arrived from Ireland, Scotland, Wales and places further afield.

The population growth in the north was most apparent in a band of land stretching from Hull in the east across the Pennines to Liverpool in the west. Hull and Liverpool developed as the ports for this huge industrial region, but it was massive towns like Manchester in Lancashire and Leeds in Yorkshire that really dominated this industrial heartland. Most of the industrial towns in this area developed as centres of textile making.

A Manchester cotton mill circa 1835.

Textile manufacturing had previously been a cottage industry concentrated in numerous industrial villages scattered throughout the Pennines. Improvements in machinery enabled the development of enormous factory-like mills that could employ many people. Many towns specialised in particular kinds of cloth or linen but in general the Lancashire textile towns came to be noted for making cotton while the Yorkshire towns were noted for the making of wool.

Textiles were not the only industry in this increasingly populous region. Engineering was also important in certain towns while coal mining was carried out in both Lancashire and Yorkshire. The Lancashire coalfield encompassed a large part of the industrial county while Yorkshire's coalfield was centred on the southern part of Yorkshire stretching from Leeds towards Sheffield. Sheffield, at the southernmost extremity of the Yorkshire region was noted for the making of iron and steel.

Dialect in Industrial Areas

The most populated part of Northern England lies in southern Lancashire, Greater Manchester and south and western Yorkshire. It is this particular populous region that is often thought to typify the north. However in more ancient times this part of the north was disputed territory between Northumbria and the Midland Kingdom of Mercia. Dialect experts note that the speech in this area is strongly influenced by the Midlands. This means that the area thought to typify the typical northern dialect might also be considered a 'North Midland' dialect speaking area.

Perhaps it is better to seek the true northern dialects in the rural areas of northern Yorkshire, Cumberland or Northumberland. It is also worth remembering that dialects in urban and industrial areas are often 'watered down' or generalised versions of the older rural dialects. Urban dialects are often the most prominent and most familiar dialects of today but are less likely to be dialects of great antiquity.

Population Growth in North Yorkshire and the North East

Outside the great industrial belt of Yorkshire and Lancashire, the remaining parts of northern England were largely rural. The vast rural expanse of northern Yorkshire including the uplands of the North York Moors and Yorkshire Dales as well as the lowland region of the Vale of York saw very little change in population. In these areas the rural folk were less affected by the changes further south and in remoter areas some people continued to speak a deeply rooted and often impenetrable dialect that could trace its roots to Viking and Anglo-Saxon times.

The same was true in the 'Lake Counties' of Cumberland and Westmorland where industrial development only occurred in coastal ports like Workington, Whitehaven and Maryport. In the far north east, most of Northumberland was untouched by the industrial age and its people continued to speak their ancient dialect, tracing its origins back to the days of the Kingdom of Northumbria.

Newcastle

The Normans built the 'New Castle' on the site of a Roman fort near the Tyne and the town developed around the castle. Newcastle was famed for the export of coal from medieval times, but in 1286 it was the leading English port for exporting leather. Newcastle received a charter sometime before 1179 and was shipping coal to London by at least 1305. In 1378 Newcastle shipped 15,000 tons of coal per year and exported coal to many parts of Europe. Newcastle's population had reached 10,000 by 1547 and it continued to grow during the 1600s and 1700s with wagon railroads bringing coal to port from the surrounding mines. By the beginning of the nineteenth century Newcastle's population was 33,000 rising to 109,000 by 1861.

Sunderland

Sunderland received a charter in 1179 from the Prince Bishop of Durham that gave its merchants similar rights to Newcastle, but Sunderland only really began to develop as a port in the 1600s. It was still a little used port in 1559 but was shipping 14,700 tons of coal a year by 1609 when the Newcastle merchants felt threatened enough to petition the king and order a levy. By the mid 1600s Sunderland was a major rival to Newcastle for the export of North Eastern coal and had managed to break Newcastle's almost monopolistic control on the North East coal trade. Sunderland merchants sided with the Parliamentarians during the Civil War. Newcastle largely supported the Royalist side.

The County of Durham and the neighbouring regions along the river estuaries of Teesside and Tyneside formed a major industrial area primarily associated with the North East coalfield. This was a region where mining had been carried out since medieval times. It was a very important coalfield because it lay so near to the sea, allowing relatively easy shipment of coal to London and the south. In the 1600s and 1700s railroads were developed here for transporting coal to the ports of the Tyne and Wear. This was a major industrial region in its own right, quite distinct from the industrial regions of western Yorkshire and southern Lancashire.

Middlesbrough Population Growth

The rapid population growth of Middlesbrough during the nineteenth century was unmatched by any other British town. Middlesbrough was still a farmstead in 1829 but was developed as a coal port by the Pease family of Darlington. During the 1840s an iron works was established in the town and was the first of many that would stimulate the population growth of Middlesbrough. It is worth recalling the population figures from Middlesbrough's nineteenth century census statistics:

1801 – 25; **1831** – 154; **1841** - 5,463; **1851** - 7,431; **1861** - 19,416; **1871** - 39,563; **1891** - 75,532; **1901** - 91,301

The population of the industrial parts of the North East expanded rapidly during the eighteenth and nineteenth century and was concentrated in the riverside towns of Sunderland and Newcastle and in the mining areas of County Durham.

At the southern extremity of this industrial region, Teesside straddled the borders of northern Yorkshire and Durham. Here the north Yorkshire town of Middlesbrough on the Tees grew very rapidly, stimulated at first by the export of coal, but further encouraged by the making of iron and

steel. Middlesbrough would see a rapid population growth more incredible than that of any other town in the history of the British Isles.

Kingston upon Hull

Hull is the chief port of Yorkshire, with a population of 300,000 and is sometimes known as 'the biggest fishing port in the world'. It was originally a little medieval fishing village called Wyke that was purchased by King Edward I in 1293 for the construction of a harbour and war base which he called Kingston-upon-Hull. For most of its history Hull's boundaries were confined to the area of the original old town and its population numbered no more than 25,000. The growth of industrial towns in West and South Yorkshire meant that Hull needed to develop bigger and better dock facilities and the town's population had rapidly expanded to more than 100,000 by 1881.

The Growth of Leeds and Bradford

Most of the huge towns of Yorkshire grew as wool making centres, but in medieval times the making of wool was under the control of powerful monasteries.

Leeds in 1868.

As the centuries passed, the weaving and spinning of wool developed steadily during the Middle Ages as a cottage industry concentrated in places like Leeds. By 1560 Leeds was showing the first signs of major growth. In the year 1600 its population had reached 4,000.

Historic view of Halifax.

Liverpool

Liverpool developed significantly as a port in the 1600s taking over the role as the north west's most important port from Chester. This was due to the increasing size of ships and the silting up of the River Dee at Chester. In the 1500s Liverpool had been a textile exporting port connected with the Lancashire-Ireland textile trade but it was still a much smaller port than Chester.

In 1649 a rebellion took place in Ireland. As a consequence, Liverpool was banned from trading with the Irish. For this reason the port was forced to concentrate its efforts in the West Indies. At this time a wide variety of commodities passed in and out of the port. However, Liverpool's population in 1660 was still no more than 1,500, rising to 6,000 by 1708. A dock was built on the Mersey in 1710 and this stimulated the town's growth. In 1773 the population was 34,407 and was 53,853 by 1790. At the turn of the nineteenth century it was the home to 77,653 people and an amazing 376,065 people by 1851. In 1901 Liverpool's population had grown to 684,947. Throughout the nineteenth century many Irish immigrants supplemented Liverpool's rapid population growth. The Irish often lived in overcrowded slums.

In this early period, woollen cloth was produced by Yorkshire clothiers who worked in cottages or in attached workshops in Leeds and surrounding villages. Towns like Leeds, Halifax and Huddersfield provided market centres for the sale of the cloth and other agricultural produce. In the eighteenth century Leeds grew very rapidly with its population of 6,000 in 1700 rising to 16,300 in 1771.

Population Growth of Northern Towns

In 1801 the Lancashire mill towns of Oldham and Blackburn each had a population of around 12,000. By 1851 Blackburn's population was 46,000 and Oldham was home to 52,000 people. Blackburn's population had risen to 108,000 in 1851. The growth of Huddersfield's population was more modest rising from 7,268 in 1801 to 30,880 in 1851. However these population growths were nothing in comparison to the Yorkshire steel towns of Sheffield and Middlesbrough. Sheffield was a long established town that already had a population of 25,000 in 1760. This had risen to 284,410 by 1881.

Middlesbrough was smaller and was nothing more than a riverside farm in 1830, but its population had risen to a phenomenal 75,532 by 1891. Northern towns continued to grow into the early part of the twentieth century and of the nine fastest growing towns in the period 1871-1911 four were in the North of England - Middlesbrough, Gateshead, South Shields and Birkenhead.

The real boom period for Leeds was brought about by the growth of the great cloth mills in the nineteenth century. The Industrial Revolution and the introduction of improved machinery made mass production possible and spurred on the growth of the mills. In 1816 Leeds was linked to the great Lancashire port of Liverpool by the completion of the Leeds and Liverpool canal. This made shipment to the Americas ever the more easy. By

1841 the population of Leeds was 88,000 and had risen to more than 300,000 by 1881.

Throughout the Middle Ages neighbouring Bradford, was also an important woollen and textile centre, but the town did not really start to grow until the nineteenth century. Bradford had a population of around 9,000 in 1760 growing steadily to 13,000 in 1801. By 1851 104,400 people lived in Bradford and the figure had surpassed a quarter of a million by 1901. The industrial growth of Bradford attracted labour from all over Europe and the British empire and Bradford is still famed as a cultural melting pot with many people of Irish, German, Italian, Eastern European, West Indian and Asian descent.

Sheffield - the steel town

Sheffield had been known for the making of Iron and steel since medieval times and was especially well known for the making of cutlery. Most production was by small traders but after the 1850s huge steel and engineering works began to emerge in the town, employing thousands of people. The invention of the Bessemer converter in 1856 enabled the production and output of steel on a huge scale and brought a massive increase in the town's population. From 1801 to 1901 the population of the town of Sheffield increased from 31,314 to 90,398, but Sheffield had expanded well beyond the original town limits and in reality its actual population was much greater, being just short of 300,000.

The Growth of Manchester

Although York undoubtedly held the title 'capital of the North' in ancient and medieval times, Manchester often claims to be the modern cultural and economic capital of the northern region. However, people in Yorkshire and the North East regard themselves as belonging to distinct regions and would not even consider Manchester to be their regional 'capital'. Nevertheless Manchester has been a focus for northern history in recent centuries and it is a city famed for its wealth of cultural institutions. When taking into account all the neighbouring towns that now form Manchester suburbs, Manchester is also undoubtedly the most populous city in the North of England.

So how did this growth come about and what were the origins of the people who contributed to the phenomenal growth of Manchester?

A fulling mill was mentioned in Manchester in 1322 and this was one of the first indications of a textile industry in the area. By the fourteenth century King Edward III was encouraging Flemish weavers from Belgium to come to England and they soon formed a community in Manchester. The Flemish were experts in the manufacture of textiles and their skills spurred on the growth of industry in the town. Manchester was located in a central and ideally humid region close to a river on the edge of the Pennines where there was a plentiful supply of wool. However Manchester was little more than a large village or small market town during the Middle Ages.

In the sixteenth century Manchester was importing flax from Ireland by which time Manchester and the neighbouring, now almost indistinguishable town of Salford were beginning to grow and prosper. The total population of the two towns was in the region of two or three thousand. John Leland who visited Manchester in 1538 called it 'the best-builded, quickest and most populous tounne in Lancashire'. Foreign immigrants continued to have a big influence on Manchester's growing cloth trade at this time. Many arrived as victims of religious persecution from the Netherlands in the sixteenth century.

By the 1640s Manchester had a population of around 5,000 but its development from a market town into a huge industrial city really took place in the 1700s. In 1721 improvements were made to the Rivers Irwell and Mersey so that much larger vessels could reach the town. The result was that Manchester became a very busy 'inland port'.

Manchester's population began to rapidly increase, rising to approximately 17,000 in 1740. The building of more canals further stimulated the city's growth. Improvements in spinning notably by Hargreaves at Blackburn in 1767 and by other pioneers like Arkwright enabled Manchester's textile output to increase.

By 1789 Manchester's population had grown to almost 50,000. Much of the incoming population is likely to have come from a rural background, from other parts of Lancashire, Cheshire, Yorkshire, the midlands and regions further away. By 1801 Manchester's population reached 70,000, growing to just short of a quarter of million in the 1840s. It passed the half a million mark in the late 1890s. Manchester's 'swallowing up' of neighbouring textile towns boosted the town's population and many local towns effectively became Manchester suburbs.

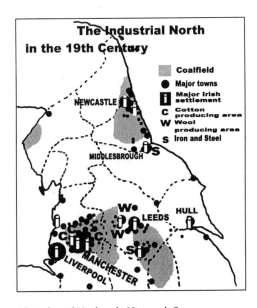

The Industrial North in the Nineteenth Century.

Although much of Manchester's expanding population would have been locally born it is estimated that on average, about one third of Manchester's 19th century population was Irish born. Irish influence in Manchester is often overlooked especially in comparison to Liverpool but the Irish influence in Manchester was every bit as strong if not stronger than in Liverpool. In fact it is estimated that around 35,000 Irish born people lived in Manchester in 1825 compared to around 24,000 in Liverpool. However, the Irish were far from being the only ethnic group represented in nineteenth century Manchester. The population included communities of Germans, Italians, French, Greeks, Arabs, Egyptians and Asians. A rich ethnic mix can still be found in Manchester to this day.

Northern England is more populous than several European nations

The industrial belt of the north of England stretching from Hull to Liverpool and encompassing Sheffield and the Yorkshire coalfield is by far the most populous part of Northern England. Over 7 million people - more than half of northern England's present day population live in this belt of land. The total population of the present North of England is around 14.5 million making it one of the most densely populated parts of Europe. In fact Northern England's total population is higher than that of several European countries including Greece, Hungary, Portugal, Sweden, Denmark, Austria, Finland, Switzerland and the Czech Republic. The population of Yorkshire alone is about the same as that of Norway.

Part Eleven:
The Irish of Northern England

Liverpool in 1830

Part Eleven:
The Irish of Northern England

The Irish Legacy

Apart from the Norman settlement of 1066, the biggest overseas influx of people into the North of England in the second millennium was undoubtedly the Irish immigration of the nineteenth century.

Of course this was an inward movement of people, from a nation that was suffering economic difficulties and was not a military, political or cultural take over like that of the Vikings and Anglo-Saxons of the first millennium. This might explain why Irish influence on the language and culture of the north was not as profound as that brought about by the invaders of the more distant past.

Normans, Vikings, and Anglo-Saxons established the political institutions; laws and place-names of our nation and the traces of their languages can still be found in the English language and dialects of the North a thousand years later. By contrast the cultural and political influence of the nineteenth century Irish is harder to distinguish, except perhaps in cases where individuals of Irish ancestry reach positions of power or cultural significance. Even when they do it often goes unnoticed because they have come to be regarded as English or Scottish or Welsh.

For example, it is unlikely that the British Prime Minister James Callaghan, who held the office from 1976 to 1979 is ever thought of as being 'ethnically Irish', despite the fact that Callaghan is undoubtedly a name of Irish origin. Similarly on the cultural front, the Liverpool born songwriters Lennon and McCartney were English because they were born and raised in England. The fact that they both have surnames of Irish origin is often overlooked. Is it not reasonable claim to their talents might have been at least partly an Irish inheritance?

The historic impact of Anglo-Saxons, Vikings and Normans upon our culture is easy to assess, as are the more recent cultural contributions of distinct ethnic groups like Asians or Afro-Caribbean. The Irish cultural legacy is sometimes overlooked, despite the fact that people of Irish origin were by far the largest ethnic group to enter northern England during the last two centuries.

With such a high number of Irish immigrants moving into Northern England in later centuries we might expect to see some Irish influence on the English language or on the local dialects of the north. We would expect there to be just as much Irish influence in the northern dialect as there is Norse Viking influence. However, Irish influence on local dialect is slight, except perhaps in Liverpool where the Irish influence is well known.

Irish immigrants were not a powerful elite like the Vikings or Normans of ancient times. There was nothing to be gained by the natives of the north if they copied or adopted aspects of Irish speech. Children of

Irish immigrants found it beneficial to adopt the local dialects of their locality in northern England, as did other newcomers from other parts of the country and the world. In any case the Irish, unlike the Anglo-Saxons of old, were always a minority, even in towns like Liverpool. In most places the Irish quickly disappeared as a distinct cultural group. Today surnames are often the only clue to the Irish origins of many a northern native.

The Irish of North West England

Irish settlement in England and particularly in the North of England has a very long history going back to the time of the Vikings and earlier. Irish immigration in the second millennium took on an even greater significance, particularly in North West England where significant Irish communities have lived since at least the fifteenth century. It is known for example that many Irish were employed on west Lancashire farms during the 1690s, although most were not permanent residents.

By the nineteenth century, census returns showed that the Irish made up a high proportion of North West England's population, with around 100,000 Irish born people living in Lancashire in 1825. Most of these Irish lived in expanding industrial towns like Liverpool and Manchester where Irish populations had started to grow long before the potato famine of 1845. Before 1845 there had been much permanent settlement of the Irish in England, partly stimulated by an earlier famine in 1801, but a very large proportion of the Irish immigration in the North West was still temporary or seasonal.

It was the Irish potato famine that really had a significant impact on the number of Irish who came to permanently settle in England. In the early nineteenth century the Irish people had come to rely heavily on the potato as a staple crop but in 1845 the crop failed as a result of a parasitic fungus. It led to widespread and increased emigration from Ireland to England, Scotland, Australia, Canada and the United States. The potato famine made the need for permanent immigration into England necessary for many Irish people and caused many Irish to emigrate much further from home.

The Irish in Liverpool

One of the first ports of call for many of the emigrating Irish was Liverpool. From there many sailed to America or found their way to other parts of Britain. Many often chose to stay in Liverpool. Here the Irish supplemented an existing Irish community that had been present in Liverpool since at least the 1600s. By 1851 Irish-born people accounted for about 25 per cent of Liverpool's population.

Liverpool in 1728.

In 1851 around 730,000 Irish-born people lived in Britain with Liverpool and Manchester being two of the four towns where Irish-born inhabitants numbered more than 50,000. In Liverpool more than 75 per cent of the dockside workers were Irish born. The other two major cities of Irish settlement in 1851 were London and Glasgow, but Lancashire was the only county in England where Irish born people made up more than 5 per cent of the population in 1851.

Irish influence in the Scouse dialect

The dialect spoken in Liverpool is called Scouse and displays both Irish and Welsh influence since Wales is also very close by. The hard TH sound becomes D in the Liverpool dialect while the soft TH becomes T. A Liverpudlian might say "Doze Tings Dere", for "Those things there". Liverpudlians may also say "tree" for "three" and this is probably of Dublin Irish origin. A 'ch' sound, similar to the 'ch' in the Scottish word loch or German word Bach is used in Liverpool in words such as 'back'. This might be Welsh rather than Irish in origin. Words with double t's are pronounced with R so that butter becomes burra and so on. In Liverpool dialects the 'air' sound might become 'ur' or vice versa. This was thought to vary between Irish Catholic and Protestant communities so that the former might say "fairly airly" whilst the latter might say "Furly Urly". The latter pronunciation is more typical of other neighbouring Lancashire dialects.

The Irish in Yorkshire and the North East

Other places that featured high in the British towns with the most Irish-born inhabitants in 1851 were Edinburgh, Dundee, Bradford, Leeds, Birmingham and Newcastle. Each of these towns had more than 7,000 Irish-born inhabitants. Another ten towns had major Irish

populations with more than 3,000 Irish-born inhabitants. These were Paisley, Sunderland, Preston, Bolton, Stockport, Hull, Sheffield, Wolverhampton, Bristol and Merthyr in Wales. The figures demonstrate that there was a particularly strong Irish influence in the North of England and Scotland. It is significant that eleven of the top twenty Irish settled towns in Britain in 1851 were in northern England while a further four were in Scotland. About 41 per cent of the Irish-born people of Britain lived in the North of England. Most of the others lived in either London or Scotland.

In the Yorkshire mill towns and colliery towns, Irish people could form a very significant proportion of the population with Yorkshire's largest Irish community living in Leeds. One observer visiting Leeds in 1849 commented that Leeds was not as overcrowded as Liverpool or Manchester. He attributed this to the Pennines, which he believed acted as a barrier to mass Irish immigration. However the Irish were arriving in Leeds in big numbers during the 1840s and 1850s. Leeds had an Irish community of some 15,000 people by 1861.

The Irish population in North East England was far behind the big cities of London, Glasgow and the North West. Nevertheless about one fifth of Tyneside's 1851 population was Irish born and another fifth were Scottish. Gateshead was home to 1,544 Irish and 1,000 Scots while nearby Sunderland was home to about 4,000 Irish and 2,300 Scots. Other parts of the region like the iron making town at Consett or the numerous colliery towns and villages of the Northumberland and Durham coalfield also attracted Irish, Scottish or Welsh labourers. As elsewhere in the country many Irishmen were employed in the construction of railways. Sometimes tensions between Irish immigrants and the native English were high, particularly in times of recession and there are several accounts of fights and even riots between Irish and English people in the nineteenth century. In some cases trouble was fuelled by religious sectarianism.

The Irish in Middlesbrough

It is noticeable that Middlesbrough and Hartlepool did not feature in the top twenty towns for Irish born residents in 1851. This was because both towns were still quite small. Hartlepool had only been transformed from a little fishing town into an industrial town in the 1840s, while Middlesbrough had been little more than a farm in 1830. By 1871 the population of Middlesbrough was still just under 40,000, but this was nevertheless a rather staggering growth in the space of only forty years.

Middlesbrough's population in 1871 was still modest in comparison to other northern towns but a significant 3,200 Middlesbrough inhabitants were Irish born. This was in addition to 1,531 Welsh, 1,368 Scots, 1,169 West Midlanders and 600 people from overseas. During the 1870s settlers from depressed agricultural regions in the east of England like East Anglia sought work in the newly expanding town of Middlesbrough.

Middlesbrough industrialists often hired these labourers at special markets. Of course a large proportion of the Middlesbrough's residents came from the North East region. However, although Middlesbrough was a Yorkshire town on the border with County Durham, a third of the town's inhabitants were born outside these two counties.

The Irish were the major immigrant group in Middlesbrough and by the late nineteenth century the proportion of Irish people in Middlesbrough population was said to be second only to Liverpool. Like many other urban and industrial regions of the north, Middlesbrough's population featured people of many other British origins including Scots, Welsh and East Anglians. A Welsh presence was especially noticeable in the iron making industry. Look at any telephone directory for Teesside, Merseyside or any other northern region and you will find dozens and dozens of surnames of Irish, Scottish and Welsh origin.

Catarrh

A person from Stockton once told me that "half the population of Middlesbrough was Irish and that the other half was Welsh". The Merseyside dialect has been described as "one third Irish, one third Welsh and one third catarrh" There may be some truth in the second of these jokey comments. In the nineteenth century many people in Merseyside and other industrial areas lived in very damp, overcrowded slums that could cause catarrh or nasal congestion. This may have had a lasting effect on the local dialect.

Where the Irish Worked

It is often stated that most Irish people in England found work as labourers and that many worked as 'navvies' - this being an abbreviation of navigator. Navvies worked on the building of roads and railways. The early nineteenth century certainly saw a massive increase in the construction of the railways and the Irish played an important part in the construction of Britain's rail network. Irish involvement in the construction of roads is also well known, but the Irish who settled in Britain were also involved in many other kinds of employment. In the coal mining areas of County Durham, Lancashire and Yorkshire many were employed as miners while those in the larger towns fulfilled many different roles of employment. A significant number were upwardly mobile enough to take on work more closely associated with the Middle Classes in towns like Manchester and Liverpool.

By 1871 census records for mainland Britain showed there to be more than half a million Irish born people. Some estimates suggest that when second generation Irish were taken into account, the figure was very much higher. An Irish - born schoolteacher called Hugh Heinrick estimated in his "Survey of the Irish in England" that there were in fact more than two and a half million Irish living in Britain in 1872. Second generation Irish were much harder to survey, since many were losing their ethnicity and spoke with local English dialects. The second generation Irish were of course Irish by parentage but not by birth.

Historic view of Manchester.

An example of the influence of second generation Irish can be found by studying surnames and nineteenth century census returns. In the 1881 census for Lancashire there are 6,969 people listed with the name Murphy. This was one of the most numerous Irish names and yet only 2,542 or 36 % of these Murphys were actually born in Ireland. Most of the others were born in Lancashire itself, with the heaviest concentrations living in Liverpool and Manchester. However, 70 % of the Lancashire Murphys over the age of 30 were born in Ireland. This suggests that most of the Murphys living in Lancashire in 1881 were the children or even grandchildren of the Murphys who had arrived from Ireland earlier in the century.

Today it is almost impossible to distinguish people of Irish origin from other people in the north. The only clues are often in the proportion of people with Irish surnames or areas where Roman Catholicism is particularly strong. Even where surnames give away a clue to an Irish background it is often overlooked in England. This is especially noticeable when compared to the United

States where having an Irish surname is likely to be accompanied by a strong emotional attachment to Ireland, even though many generations of the family may have lived in America.

Irish O' Names

Many Irish workers came to live in the North in the nineteenth century so Irish surnames are common throughout northern England. The O' in many of these Irish surnames denoted a clan group or 'sept' in more ancient times. Many of these names trace their origin to the eleventh century or earlier. O' means ' descendant of' and names like O' Connor, O'Brien and O'Neil originally had a Celtic spelling.

In Ireland most of these names were later given English spellings. Some Irish surnames also dropped the initial O' because of English influence. For example the Irish surname O'Ceileachain became O'Callaghan and in many cases was shortened to Callaghan. In a similar way O'Suileabhain became Sullivan, while Ryan and Byrne were originally O'Riain and O'Byrne. More surprising is the name O' Murchadha - meaning descendant of the sea-warrior. This became O'Murphy. It looks like a strange transformation but the name reflects the Irish pronunciation and now simply occurs as Murphy, one of the most numerous Irish names. Similarly the name Collins comes from O' Cullane, whilst Kelly is from O'Ceallaigh meaning 'descendant of war'. Kennedy is from O'Cinneide, meaning 'ugly head'.

Irish 'Mac' Names

The word Mac occurs in Irish surnames like McDermott (McDiarmada), McCaffrey, McNamara and McLoughlin. As with the Gaelic names of Scotland, Mac means 'descendant of' or 'son of'. It is probable that the earliest Scots, who came from Ulster in Ireland, imported the Mac prefix into Scotland. Centuries later in Cromwellian times, many Scots settled in Northern Ireland and some Mac surnames were imported back into Ireland. Mac surnames in Ireland could therefore be of either Irish or Scottish origin.

Welsh and Scots

The Welsh and Scottish immigration into England was not as great as that of the Irish and is often overlooked. Apart from the Irish, the Welsh and Scots were the major immigrant community in the northern counties from outside England. However, in 1881 the combined number of Welsh and Scottish born people living in the northern counties was never as high as that of the Irish. The Border County of Northumberland was the only northern county where the number of Scottish born residents significantly exceeded those who were Irish born. Westmorland also had more Scots born than Irish, but here the population was very small and largely rural. Cumberland, like Northumberland a Border County, had a similar proportion of Scots to the proportion of Irish born in its population, but even here the Irish exceeded the number of Scots. Welsh populations were most noticeable in Lancashire and Cheshire, where Welsh communities were already significant at the beginning of the nineteenth century.

Until the 1830s, when industrial growth and the development of towns dramatically increased, people with Welsh surnames were concentrated in Wales and the Welsh border counties of England like Cheshire and Shropshire. Most people in Wales, as in rural England were largely employed in agriculture, but when nearby English towns began to develop as a result of industrial growth, the better wages attracted many Welsh into towns like Birmingham and Liverpool. Gradually Welsh people would move into other industrial areas of the north and today people with Welsh surnames are numerous throughout the northern region. Some Welsh, particularly those from south Wales were experienced in the iron and coal industry and found work in these fields in parts of England. Counties like Durham would attract significant numbers of Welsh.

Welsh surnames

Over the centuries many Welsh people have settled in England and Welsh surnames are numerous in the North. Welsh surnames are often based on a Christian name. Examples include Williams, Thomas, Davis (David), Richards, Hughes and Edwards while the surnames Jones and Evans both derive from John.

Welsh surnames developed quite late, since the Welsh traditionally did not use surnames. Instead they took the forenames of their fathers, as part of their name in a similar fashion to the Vikings. Surnames became fixed in Wales in the 1600s, 1700s and in some cases as late as the 1800s, when many Welsh had names like Williams or Richards. The name Richards meant 'son of Richard', having the same meaning as the English surname Richardson. The Normans had introduced forenames like Richard, John and William into Wales and these had become popular as forenames in Wales in the 1600s. Some Welsh surnames like Griffiths are based on older Celtic forenames that had been used in Wales long before the Norman Conquest. Many Welsh surnames were originally prefixed with 'Ap or Ab' meaning 'son of'. This was often dropped in later times or clipped, so surnames like Ap Rhys, meaning 'son of Rhys' became Price, while Ap Hugh - son of Hugh became Pugh and ab Evan son of Evan became Bevan. Not all Welsh surnames derive from Christian names. The Welsh surname Lloyd comes from the Welsh word 'llwyd' meaning grey. It probably means grey-haired and is widespread in England. However we need to be cautious, as evidence shows that some apparently Welsh names like Roberts, Richards and even Lloyd developed separately in both Wales and England. Generally there isn't as great a variety of Welsh surnames as there are surnames of Irish, Scottish or English origin. It is estimated that there are only 39 common Welsh surnames and these are used by 95% of all Welsh people.

A study of Welsh surnames in Lancashire in the 1881 census demonstrates that people of Welsh origin were well established in this particular county during the late nineteenth century. Records show that there were more than 5,300 Griffiths, 18,400 Williamses, 7,300 Edwards and 34,800 people with the surname Jones. Approximately fifty per cent of the people in Lancashire with these surnames were born in Lancashire, particularly in the larger cities like Liverpool and Manchester. Many were also born in Welsh border counties like Cheshire and Shropshire and nearby industrialised midland counties like Staffordshire. Less than a third of the Lancashire people with Welsh surnames of this kind were actually born in Wales.

Scottish born immigrants were also attracted to northern England in large numbers. Northumberland, which included the industrial city of Newcastle upon Tyne had the highest proportion of Scottish born people of all the northern counties in 1881, probably because of the county's proximity to the Scottish border. Scots accounted for 4.94% of Northumberland's population or approximately 21,000 people.

Lancashire was the home to 52,000 Scots-born people in 1881, although this only accounted for about 1.5% of the county's overall population. As with the Welsh and Irish, such figures do not take account of second generation Scots.

For example, there were 4,230 Macdonalds and 947 McKenzies living in Lancashire in 1881, but most of these were born in Lancashire rather than

Scotland. Only a quarter of the Lancashire Mckenzies and as little as a tenth of the Lancashire MacDonalds had been born in Scotland. Most of the other MacDonalds were born in other parts of England. This suggests that this particular Scottish surname had become very well established south of the border by 1881.

Where people were born in 1881

County (including the names of some major towns)	% Born in the County	% Born in other Northern Counties	% Born in Ireland	% Born in Scotland or Wales	% Born Elsewhere (mostly in England)	Total Population
Cheshire (Birkenhead, Stockport)	63%	13% (10.5% born in Lancashire)	4%	2%	18%	645,072
Cumberland (Carlisle, Workington)	75%	9% (3.6% born in W'land or Lanc)	6%	5%	5%	251,582
Co. Durham (Gateshead, Sunderland, Stockton)	64%	16% (13% born in N'land or Yorks)	4%	3%	13%	869,486
Lancashire (Manchester, Liverpool)	67%	9% (7% born in Yorkshire and Cheshire)	6%	2%	16%	3,467,851
Northumberland	60%	13% 8% born in Co. Durham)	3%	5%	20%	434,797
Westmorland	72%	20% (Most born in Lancashire, Cumberland and Yorkshire)	1%	2%	5%	64,209
Yorkshire (Leeds, Bradford, Hull, Middlesbrough)	78%	4% (Most born in Lancs 2.5% or Durham 1.2%)	2%	1%	15%	2,895,481

Part Twelve:
Around the World in the North

Liverpool has a long multi-cultural history

numbers. However it is worth looking at some of the major ethnic groups to have settled in the north during the centuries of the second millennium.

Part Twelve:
Around the World in the North

Immigration from around the World

We have seen that Irish immigration in northern England has taken place over many centuries and in some cases the Irish could make up to a quarter of the population of certain northern towns during the nineteenth century. Scots and Welsh have also contributed significantly to the population, as did people from English counties in the midlands and south. However immigration from overseas did not come solely from Ireland.

People from many corners of the world came to settle in Britain during the second millennium, arriving from the continents of Europe, Asia and Africa. Many diverse cultural groups settled in northern England with many different religions and languages. Poles, Jews, Indians, Sikhs, Pakistanis, Africans, Jamaicans, Germans and Chinese are included in the vast range of cultural groups that have settled in the north of England in varying degrees. Some arrived in recent decades in the post war period, while others arrived many centuries earlier. It is not possible to cover all these groups adequately in a book of this size and some cultural groups have only settled in very small

Jewish influence in the North

Jewish settlement in Northern England can be traced back to medieval times. The Diaspora or dispersion of Jews from Palestine began in 586 BC after the Babylonians conquered Judah. Over the centuries major centres of Jewish population moved from country to country often adopting the local languages while retaining Jewish customs and practices.

Centres of Jewish Diaspora included Spain, France, Germany, Poland and Russia but England was one of the last countries in Europe to see major Jewish settlement. Jewish immigrants did not begin to arrive in England until shortly after the Norman Conquest. This was particularly the case after 1100 when the Berbers were driving the Jews out of Spain.

Jews were severely restricted in medieval business and were excluded from Christian craft guilds. For this reason many Jews turned to money lending. Unfortunately, as people accumulated debts many Jews were resented for their money-lending activities. Throughout the medieval period, incidents of Jewish persecution increased, often supported by untruthful rumours that Jews practised the ritual sacrifice of children. At York on March 16, 1190, over one hundred and fifty Jews took refuge in Clifford's Tower after riots broke out. The Jews were ordered to convert to Christianity or die. Many chose suicide or were killed as they tried to escape.

By the 13th Century anti-Jewish feeling had reached a height and Italians in England became known as an alternative source of money lending. In 1290 Edward I made it illegal for Jews to live in England - a law that remained in force until the time of Oliver Cromwell in the 1650s. In the late 1600s Jews began to settle in England from central Europe, Spain, Portugal and North Africa, although most of the early settlements in this period were in the south coast ports. Persecution of Jews in central Europe in the 1700s brought further Jewish settlement in the expanding industrial towns of the north. From around 1740 Jewish communities appeared in major northern towns like Manchester, Leeds and Liverpool, appearing in the North East at Sunderland around 1781.

Many Jews arrived in the North of England at Hull where many chose to settle. Most were destined for Liverpool, where they could take a journey towards the New World. However many stayed in the north of England, where they found they could utilise their skills and expertise as tailors in the textile trades of towns in Lancashire and Yorkshire. Many stayed in the port of Liverpool.

Jewish settlement from Russia and central Europe continued in the nineteenth century and early twentieth century. This further increased the Jewish populations of the North. Many Jews were renowned for their expertise in retailing and the clothing industry and were a significant ethnic group in the textile towns of Leeds and Manchester. There were around 10 Jewish families living in Leeds in 1841 but this had increased to 6,000 individuals by the 1880s, with most working in the textile industry in workshops rather than factories. Many Jews were concentrated in the Leylands district of the town. Manchester's Jewish community dates back to the 1740s and today there are around 28,000 Jewish people living in the city.

Mr Marks and Mr Spencer

Jews were often noted for their skills in retailing. These included Michael Marks, a Lithuanian Jew who landed at the port of Stockton on Tees during the nineteenth century. He settled in Leeds where he began trading in 1884 with his own 'penny bazzar store' where everything cost a penny. He later moved to Wigan in Lancashire where he teamed up with a Yorkshireman from Skipton called Tom Spencer. Their partnership developed into one of Britain's most famous retailing companies Marks & Spencer.

Gypsies in the North

Gypsies, a travelling people, are said to have arrived in Europe around 1418 where they were mistakenly identified as 'Egyptian'. The word 'gypsy' derives from Egyptian. Gypsies spoke a non-European language known today as 'Romany'. It is a language most closely related to Sanskrit, the classical language of the Indian subcontinent. Studies have shown that Romany belongs to group of languages called 'Indo-Iranian' but Romany is most closely related to the languages of North-West India. Most Romany words are of Sanskrit origin, but some words are borrowed from other Asian and European languages, this being a legacy of their wide travelling history.

Gypsies are believed to have left India around 1000 AD and appeared in Europe by the 15th Century, soon spreading to England. Some gypsies travelled extensively in the north of England and one clan of gypsies called the Faas or Faws were very closely associated with the Northumberland-Scotland border, particularly in the region of Kirk Yetholm. They are said to have saved the life of an influential Yetholm resident who granted them residence in the town. It is also possible that they lived on the Border to escape persecution, being able to escape the laws of Scotland or England by fleeing across the border. In fact it is said that Gypsies stole horses in England and sold them in Scotland and vice versa. However, livestock thieving was very much a way of life amongst all Border people in times gone by.

The gypsy presence may have had some influence upon the dialect of Berwick upon Tweed further down the valley. A presentation to the fourth International Conference of Romany Linguistics at Manchester University in 1998 demonstrated that Romany words were still quite prominent in Berwick, particularly amongst children.

Most of the gypsies in Northumberland and the Scottish Borders seem to have adopted English and Scottish surnames. Gypsies are recorded with surnames like Baliol, Baillie, Winter, Keith, Yorkston, Shawe, Anderson, Grey, Halliday, Robertson, Wilson, Stewart, Geddes and Wilkie. The four gypsy clans of Yetholm near the Northumberland-Scotland border were Douglas, Young, Faa and Blyth. One author who visited Yetholm in the late ninth century described the first three of these families as having dark complexions with black hair. The Blyths were described as fair haired and light skinned. The Faas also known as the Faws were considered to be gypsy 'aristocracy' and a number of their clan were crowned Gypsy Kings and Queens. Their surname derives from an old Anglo-Saxon word 'falwe' (fallow) and is thought to mean 'sallow skinned'.

Gypsies and Gadgies

One Romany word familiar in the northern counties is 'Gadgie' meaning 'man' and often means 'old man'. The word is used in Cumbria, lowland Scotland, Tyneside, Durham and Teesside but may have spread south from the Borders. In Romany it was spelt 'Gage' or 'Gorgio' and originally meant any person of non-gypsy origin.

The African-Caribbean Legacy

Evidence for the very early presence of African people in Northern England is only slight. It is however known that North Africans garrisoned forts along Hadrian's Wall in Roman times. It is also known that the Vikings often came into contact with Africans. The Vikings sold Irish slaves to Africa and perhaps some Africans found themselves enslaved and brought to England or Ireland by the far travelling Norsemen.

A continuous African presence is thought to have existed in England since at least the 1500s, but it is likely that most of this population was concentrated in London. The real beginnings of African settlement in the north started in the 1700s, when many Africans arrived in England as a result of the slave trade. The transportation of African slaves was associated with the so-called 'Triangular Trade'. This involved merchants sailing from England and then travelling to the coast of western Africa where slaves were bought in exchange for goods from native African slave traders. These slaves were then transported to the Caribbean islands and America. The slave trade was a brutal process and the journey from Africa to the Caribbean could take six to eight weeks. As many as thirty per cent of the slaves might die during the journey to the West Indies. Upon landing, the Africans were sold to tobacco, coffee or sugar plantations whose owners were wealthy Caribbean families of British or European origin.

The enslaved Africans who were taken to the Caribbean came from many different African tribes and nations. They spoke many different languages and had many different cultures. In the Caribbean islands these cultural groups were not considered. Enslaved families were often broken up, making it difficult for the various African languages and cultures to survive. The

Africans learned English and gradually over time a distinct Afro-Caribbean culture and dialect of English developed.

After selling the slaves in the Caribbean, the English slave trading merchants returned home to England on the third leg of their triangular journey. A small number of Africans were transported on this third leg and brought to England to work as servants in wealthy households. The slave traders often employed slaves in their own English households. Owning an African servant was seen as a sign of great status.

Many African males also found themselves sold to British sea captains to become sailors. In fact it has been suggested that up to a quarter of all British sailors in the eighteenth century were black. This may have helped the black population to become widespread throughout Britain, as some settled in coastal ports. Indeed during the eighteenth century scattered black populations could be found almost everywhere as far north as Fife in Scotland.

Africans and Liverpool

Liverpool was the most important slave trading port in England, having eclipsed both London and Bristol during the 1700s. By 1792 Liverpool accounted for 42 per cent of European slave trading. Many black servants found themselves employed as servants by wealthy Liverpool families and in neighbouring parts of the north. There was an African presence in the population of Liverpool from the early 1700s with the sons of West African leaders often being educated in the town. Manchester had a significant black population by the middle of the eighteenth century while in London there was a community of some 20,000 Africans by the 1760s, possibly accounting for more than half of the African population of Britain as a whole.

In 1784 many Blacks who had served in the British army during the American War of Independence began to settle in England, and particularly in Liverpool and London. It is believed that around 20 per cent of the British army were black. A similar percentage had been fighting on the American side.

In the late 1700s, the rights of slave owners were gradually eroded until slavery was finally abolished in Britain in 1806. Nevertheless many Africans would continue to be employed as servants, in wealthy households. Often black servants intermarried with white servants and over time people of mixed racial origin could be found. This still has a surprising legacy today and on occasions some families in places like Liverpool have been surprised to discover that their family includes a black African ancestor who lived in say the early part of the nineteenth century.

Afro-Caribbeans in the Post War Period

It is impossible to know how many people living in the nineteenth century North of England were of African descent. Census returns during the nineteenth century did not give details of racial origin. Surnames, which are often useful for tracing people with Irish, Scottish, Welsh, Asian or Jewish origin give us no clue to African origins. There were no distinct surnames associated with the black population in Britain. This is yet another legacy of the days of slave trading, when the Africans were stripped of their names and identity and had to take on the British surnames of the families who owned them.

However the most important thing to realise is that the black presence in England was already significant prior to the twentieth century. It is often mistakenly believed that people of African origin only arrived in Britain during the middle part of the twentieth century. Certainly, the most significant influx of black people was during the Second World War when many Black people arrived in Britain from the Caribbean. Many were employed to maintain the wartime infrastructure, finding employment in health, transport and the manufacture of armaments. Around 8,000 African-Caribbeans had fought in the British forces.

Many of these people chose to settle in Britain with their families after the war, adding further to the existing black communities in the towns and cities of the north. Today there are more than half a million people of African or West Indian origin living in Britain with several thousand living in northern towns and cities like Leeds, Bradford, Huddersfield, Sheffield, Manchester and Liverpool.

Asian Communities

Asians have formed an element in England's population since at least the early eighteenth century. Indian visitors and residents in Britain during this early period included students, tourists and domestic servants. The Indian presence in Britain was closely related to British Imperialism. This was also the case with the Chinese. Hong Kong in China had come under the control of the British Empire in 1842 whilst India had come under British rule from 1857. Even before this time, British companies had held considerable power in India during the eighteenth century.

Many Indian and Chinese labourers worked for the British Empire in Asia and were employed in docks, plantations, ships and on the railways. Chinese men were often employed as sailors, usually working in the laundry trade while at sea. Many Chinese continued to pursue this trade after settling in Britain. Chinese settlement was initially concentrated in the ports and the first and oldest Chinese community in Europe was established at Liverpool, with particular growth after 1865. The establishment of the Blue Funnel steam ship line between

Liverpool and China helped to stimulate this growth. However, the Chinese communities of nineteenth century Britain were generally quite small.

Indian and other Asian communities were also relatively small in nineteenth century Britain. The most significant influx of Asian immigrants occurred during the twentieth century. During the First World War more than half a million Indians of different creeds fought for the British on the fields of Flanders. After the war, many de-mobbed Indian soldiers settled in England, often finding work in the industrial regions of the north. The same was true after the Second World War during which period as many as 2.6 million Indians fought for the British.

Events in India during 1947 further increased the number of Indians entering the country. In that year India became independent of Britain and the Indian sub continent was divided up, with the creation of the Muslim nations of Pakistan and Bangladesh in the North and the mostly Hindu nation of India in the south.

India's division resulted in significant disruptions and movement of population in the border regions of the Indian sub continent where many people had no choice but to leave their homes. Disruption was particularly noticeable in the Punjab region that stretched into both India and Pakistan. In Pakistan most Punjabis were

Muslims while those in the Punjab region of India were Sikhs or Hindus.

From 1947 many people of different religious backgrounds settled in the North of England from Asia, with a large majority originating from the Punjab region. Today the Indian community in Britain is close to a million people and a great many are from the Punjab. Sikhs are particularly numerous in the West Yorkshire towns of Bradford, Huddersfield and Leeds. Britain's Pakistani community is more than half a million strong and again most originate from the Punjab. Bradford has a particularly large community of Pakistanis.

Although most Muslims in the North are of Asian origin, a smaller number are of African or Middle Eastern origin. The longest established Muslim communities in the UK originate from the Yemen and neighbouring Somalia. Many of these people came to Britain as seamen following the opening of the Suez Canal in 1869.

They formed Muslim communities in English coastal ports like Liverpool, Hull and South Shields. The Muslim community of South Shields developed around 1870 and lived in an area known locally as the 'Arab Quarter'. Many of its inhabitants had been stokers working on steamships in the North Sea.

Compared to the Muslim and Asian communities, Britain's Chinese community is relatively small, totalling around 150,000. Major Chinese communities in the north can be found in Manchester, Liverpool and Newcastle. The Chinese communities saw considerable expansion during the 1950s and 1960s when the British taste for Chinese food encouraged many Chinese people from Hong Kong to open restaurants in the towns and cities of the north.

A Dialect Glossary

Northern dialects display many features going back to Anglo-Saxon and Viking times. Of course dialects are beginning to die out and many words are no longer used, but here are some of the more familiar dialect words.

Abaht/Aboot: In the West Riding of Yorkshire abaht was the word for 'About'. The traditional dialect word in Northumberland, Durham and North Yorkshire was 'Aboot'. The Anglo-Saxon word was on-butan.

Addle: Yorkshire word meaning to earn. Of Old Norse origin.

Afooare: Yorkshire word for Before. From the Anglo-Saxon onforan.

Aht: The West Yorkshire word for out. See also Oot.

Amang: Northern dialect for among. It is a word of Anglo-Saxon origin.

Arran: Yorkshire word of Old French origin for a spider.

Ashington Dialect: Ashington is located in the mining district of south east Northumberland and is noted for its particularly strong dialect. In the Ashington dialect Turtle means total,

Sex means Sacks and a Skirt is a native of Scotland.

Aud/Auld/Ald/Awd: Northern forms of the word old, from the Anglo-Saxon Eald. In West Yorkshire and Lancashire the word is Owd.

Axe: Northern word for ask, from the Anglo-Saxon 'Acsian'.

Aye: Northern word for Yes. Probably from an Old Norse and Germanic word Ey meaning 'always'.

Bairn/Barn: Northern English and Scottish word for a Child. In Anglo-Saxon it was Bearn. In Icelandic, Norwegian, Danish and Swedish it is Barn.

Bait: A Northern word for food or a snack that is taken to work. The word was especially popular amongst North East miners. It comes from the Scandinavian Beita and Middle English Beyten.

Beck: A Viking word for a stream commonly used in all the northern English counties except Northumberland and Lancashire.

Beor: Northern English word for Beer. In Anglo-Saxon it was Beor. In Dutch it is Bier in Icelandic it is Bjor.

Bigg: Old Northern word for barley, from a Scandinavian word. One of the historic streets in Newcastle is known as the Bigg Market.

Blinnd: A Yorkshire word for Blind, pronounced with a short I.

Boggle: A northern word for a ghost or spectre. It is probably of Celtic origin, deriving from the old Welsh Bwg. It is related to the phrase Bogie Man.

Bonny: A northern word meaning Beautiful or Pretty, from the French Bon.

Breeks/Britches: A Northern word for Breeches (Trousers), from the Anglo-Saxon word Broec. In Yorkshire the word is Breeaks.

Breed: Northern word for bread. Anglo-Saxon in origin.

Brock: A northern word for Badger, it is of Celtic origin.

Burn: An old Anglo-Saxon word for a stream now used mainly in Scotland, Northumberland and parts of County Durham.

Burr: The name given to the strange pronunciation of the 'R' sound in Northumberland. It was possibly introduced for fashionable reasons in the fourteenth century from France. It sounds a little bit like a W. One theory is that it is an imitation of the fourteenth century Northumbrian hero Harry Hotspur who had difficulty pronouncing the R sound. It is quite different from the trilled R sound of Scottish dialects.

Byeuk: The North East word for a book.

Canny: A versatile word in the North East of England - "Canny old soul" - nice old person. "Canny good/hard" - very good/tough. "Gan canny" - go carefully/slowly. Elsewhere canny is used exclusively to mean shrewd. The word may be related to the Scottish word Ken.

Carr: Woodland or scrubland with marsh. From the Old Norse Kjarr.

Chare: A word for an alley or narrow lane, often used in the North East. It comes from the Anglo-Saxon Cerra meaning 'to turn.'

Claes/Clathes: Scottish and northern word for clothes of Anglo-Saxon origin. Cleeas is a North Yorkshire variation of the word.

Clag/Claggy: Northern word for stick/sticky. From a Scandinavian word Klag.

Clarty: North East and Cumbrian word for muddy. Probably derives from clag.

Cleg: In Yorkshire, a horse fly from the Old Norse kleggi.

Coble: A fishing boat. Word is probably of Welsh/Celtic origin, from Ceubal/Cwrwgle or perhaps from the Anglo-Saxon Cuopa.

Clough: In northern place-names this is a ravine. The surname clough is of Yorkshire origin.

Clout/Cloot: In the North East and North Yorkshire the word for a rag or cloth. A word of Scandinavian or Anglo-Saxon origin. In West Yorkshire the word is Claht.

Coo: North East word for a Cow. It is an Anglo-Saxon pronunciation.

Cowp: Northern word meaning overturn. Of Scandinavian origin.

Craa: A northern word for a Crow. In Anglo-Saxon it was Crawe. In Frisian – 'Krie', Danish – 'Krage', In Dutch – 'Kraaj'.

Crack: In the North this word can mean 'to talk'. It is related to a Dutch word Kraaken. It is also used in Ireland for good, fun, company and conversation.

Cuddy: In the North East and North Yorkshire a Cuddy is a Donkey. Named after St. Cuthbert, the famous Northumbrian saint. Elsewhere donkeys were called Neddys after St Edward.

Cuddy Wifter: One of several northern words for left handed. Others include Cak-handed and Carr-handed.

Cushat: A Northern word for a pigeon or dove, from the Anglo-Saxon Cuscute.

Dee: The North East word for 'Do'.

Deed: A northern dialect word for Dead - the old Anglo-Saxon and Middle English word for Dead was Dede.

Dene: An Anglo-Saxon name for a small valley.

Divvent: Geordie for "do not". In Sunderland and Durham the word is Dinnut.

Dunsh: An old Germanic word meaning to bash into. It is used as a word in the North of England.

Dutch: Dutch influence is sometimes found in northern dialects and paticulalrly in Tyneside. This may have historic connections with Newcastle's heyday as a seaport, when Holland was one of the most powerful maritime nations. However Dutch is quite closely related to other older languages like Anglo-Saxon, Old Norse and Frisian.

Fash: Northern word. To be fashed is to be bothered /motivated. A word of old French origin.

Fell: A common northern word for a hill or a mountain. From the Old Norse Fjall.

Femmer: Cumbrian and North East word meaning weak/fragile. From the Old Norse Fimr.

Gadgie: A person. A word of Romany origin. In Yorkshire the word is gadge.

Gan: From Gangan or Gan, an Anglo-Saxon word for 'go' still used in Scotland and the North. It was also known to the Vikings.

Ganzie: North East word for a jumper or sweater. Named after the island of Guernsey.

Garth: From the Old Norse or Germanic Gardr/Garten meaning Yard/Enclosure. This often occurs in Northern place-names.

Gate: An old word for a road or way. It is a Norse word.

Gaumless/Gormless: A northern word for "Stupid"or "Useless" It is of Viking origin and has given rise to the river-name Gaunless in County Durham.

Gawp: Yorkshire word meaning to stare. From the Old Norse 'Gapa'.

Geordies: The name given to Tynesiders, especially those from Newcastle. In earlier times it seems to have been more broadly applied to coal miners from all parts of Northumberland and Durham. It comes from Geordie, a northern and Scottish nickname for George and may refer to the coal miners' use of George Stephenson's miners' safety lamp. One theory connecting Newcastle with Geordie is that the town supported the claims of George I to the English throne when the rest of Northumberland declared its support for James Stuart, the 'Old Pretender' in the Jacobite Rising of 1715. The Northumbrians are said to have labelled the Newcastle folk 'Geordies'.

Gill: This widespread northern surname may come from the Old Norse Gilli or Old Irish Gilla, both meaning 'servant'. It could also come from the Old Norse word Gill, meaning a ravine.

Glower: Northern word meaning to stare. From the Old Norse Glora.

Gob: A commonly used word for a mouth. It is thought to be of Celtic origin.

Gowk: A northern word for a Cuckoo. From the Anglo-Saxon Goec, or Scandinavian, Goek.

Hadaway: A Tyneside phrase with a nautical origin.

Happen: In Yorkshire can mean 'perhaps' or 'maybe' from the Old Norse 'Happ'.

Hinny: The pronounciation of Honey (a term on endearment) in North East England.

Hope: In place-names this is a side valley. It is of Anglo-Saxon origin and is pronounced 'up. The place-name Stanhope in County Durham means 'Stony Valley'.

Hoppen: A fair. From an Anglo-Saxon and Old German word.

Hoy: A North East word meaning 'to throw'. Possibly of Dutch origin.

Hull Dialect: Hull is the main industrial town of the East Riding of Yorkshire. It has some similarities to other dialects of industrial Yorkshire. The word work is pronounced Wairk as in Middlesbrough - the main industrial town of the old North Riding.

Hunkers: Sitting on haunches, a phrase traditionally used by North East miners. It derives from the Dutch Huicken, German Hocken, or old Norse Hokra (to crouch).

Hyem/Hyem: North East and Cumbrian word for home. Probably from the Scandinavian word Hiem.

Ice-shoggles: Old Yorkshire word for icicles from the Old Norse, isjukel.

Jamie: An old name for a collier ship from Wearside. The Sunderland sailors were also called Jamies. Geordie was a name given to a collier ship from the Tyne. The name Jamie seems to have been a kind of insult and may have referred to Scots in the Sunderland population. It could also imply that Sunderland supported James Stuart in the Jacobite Rising of 1715, but there is no evidence to confirm this. In the 1600s Sunderland took opposing sides to Newcastle in the Civil War when many of the Scots who besieged Newcastle were based at Sunderland.

Keld: In Cumbria and Yorkshire means a spring or well. From the Old Norse, Kelda.

Keek: A north eastern and Cumbrian word meaning to peep. It may be of Dutch origin Kijken or from the Swedish Kika.

Keel: A boat from the Anglo-Saxon word Ceol.

Ken: Scots word for ' know'. In Frisian the word is Kenne, in Danish Kende and in Norwegian Kjenne. In North East England the dialect word is Knaa.

Ket: A Northern word from the Viking Kjett meaning discarded 'flesh'. It usually meant 'rubbish' or 'not nice'. In County Durham it usually means a 'sweet', probably because parents reprimanded their children telling them that sweets were 'ket' - that is not good for them.

Kist: Northern word for a chest or trunk from the Old Norse, Kista.

Lad: Northern word for a boy. An Anglo-Saxon word.

Laik/Lake: Means to play in Durham, Yorkshire and Cumbria. It is a Norse word.

Lancashire dialect: Lancashire takes its name from the town of Lancaster which is ultimately named after the River Lune. Many linguistic experts regard the Lancashire speech as a West

Midland dialect rather than a Northern dialect. Distinct versions of Lancashire speech are spoken in Liverpool (Scouse) and Manchester. See also Post vocalic 'R'.

Larn: In northern dialects larn means 'teach' as in the Geordie "A'll larn yer" (I'll teach you). In Anglo-Saxon the word Laeran actually meant 'to teach'.

Lass: A common northern term for a woman or young girl. From a Scandinavian word Laskr.

Law: Often pronounced Laa. A flat-topped hill often, from the Anglo-word - Hlaw. Place-names include Tow Law, Warden Law, Hare Law. Laws are often associated with ancient sites.

Lop: In northern dialects, a flea (See loup).

Loup: A northern word for Leap. It is a word of Viking origin.

Mackem: Nicknames given to people from Sunderland/Wearside. A similar name Mac N' Tac was also once applied to County Durham. It comes from the localised dialect pronunciation of Make and Take and in Sunderland's case is thought to refer to the building of ships. "We mackem, you tackem". As with the term Geordie, no one seems to be certain, but like Geordie it may have started out as an insult or jibe.

Mair: Northumbrian and Scottish word for more. In Anglo-Saxon it was Mara. In Frisian it was Mear, Danish Mere, Dutch Meer, Swedish Mer.

Marra: In the North East a marra is a workmate. A word once commonly used by coal miners.

Mercian dialect: Anglo-Saxon dialect of central England. It had an important influence on the development of English. This was primarily because it was spoken in the influential cities of Oxford, Cambridge and London. The Mercian dialect was spoken as far north as the southerly parts of Lancashire and Yorkshire.

Nay: Yorkshire for No. From the Old Norse Nei.

Neb: A northern word for a nose. It is an Anglo-Saxon word.

Neet: Northern English and Scots for Night. From the Anglo-Saxon Neaht, Frisian and Dutch Nacht, Danish Nat, Norwegian and Swedish Natt.

Netty: Geordie word for a toilet / WC. It also occurs in Cumbria and Yorkshire as Nessy and probably derives from 'necessary'.

Norse: The Vikings and their language (Old Norse). Can be used for Danes as well as Norwegians, but usually refers to the Norwegians.

Norse: In Geordie dialect a Norse is a Nurse. A Norseman could be a male nurse.

Nowt: Northern word for nothing from the Anglo-Saxon word Naht.

Oot: A northern word for 'Out' which derives from the Anglo-Saxon word, 'Ut'.

Ower/O'er: Northern pronunciation of over.

Peth: A steeply inclined hill, often with a road, from the Anglo-Saxon word Poeth. Examples include Morpeth in Northumberland or Framwellgate Peth in Durham.

Pitmatic: A name sometimes given to the dialects in the former coal mining areas of County Durham.

Post-vocalic R: A strong R sound pronounced after vowels. It is most noticable in south western England, but also occurs in certain parts of Lancashire like Preston and Rochdale where they might pronounce the name Burnley as if it were BuRRnley. Americans and Scots also use the post vocalic R. Most English people do not actually pronounce the letter R when it follows a vowel, although most probably think that they do.

Sackless: A North East word meaning simple/innocent/useless. Related to the Anglo-Saxon words Sacleas, Icelandic Saklaus, Swedish Saklos.

Sang: A Geordie word for a song. An Anglo-Saxon word.

Scouse dialect: The dialect spoken in Liverpool. It displays Irish and possibly Welsh influence. The hard TH sound becomes D in the Liverpool dialect while the soft TH becomes T. A Liverpudlian might say "Doze Tings Dere", for "Those things there". Liverpudlians may also say "tree" for "three" and this is almost certainly of Dublin Irish origin. A 'ch' sound similar to the 'ch' in the Scottish word loch or German word Bach is used in Liverpool words like back. Words with double t's are pronounced with R so that butter becomes burra and so on. In Liverpool dialects the 'air' sound might become 'ur' or vice versa. Pronunciation can vary between Irish Catholic and Protestant communities so that the former might say "fairly airly" whilst the latter might say "Furly Urly".

Scousers: Liverpudlians are called Scousers after a kind of broth called Labscause. This was a dish of German or Scandinavian origin similar to Irish Stew and was once popular in the area. Sailors in the area were often known as Lobscousers.

Scrogg: A northern name for a small wood. From the Viking word, Skog.

Spelk: A splinter. From the Anglo-Saxon word Spelc or Scandinavian spjelke.

Staith: A Viking word originally meaning landing place. In the north east coalfield it was a pier used for loading coal onto ships.

Stane: Northern word for Stone. In Anglo-Saxon Stan, Frisian Stiennen, Danish Sten, Dutch Steen, Norwegian Stein, Swedish Sten.

Steean: A Yorkshire pronunciation of stone.

Stob: A Northern word of Scandinavian origin meaning stump or gibbet.

Strang: Northern word of Anglo-Saxon origin meaning strong.

Teem: Northern word of Scandinavian origin meaning to pour.

Teesside Dialect: Spoken around Middlesbrough and quite different from the Tyneside dialect forty miles to the north. One good way tell the difference between the speech of a Tynesider and a Teessider is to compare the Teesside phrase."Me farther wairks in the wairks in a dairty pairple shairt mekking gairders with me Uncle Bairt" with the Tyneside phrase "Me Da warks in the warks in a dorty porple short myekin' gorders wi' wor Uncle Bort". Some Teessiders use a 'ch' sound similar to the ch in the Scottish word loch. It occurs in words like back, but is is not as obvious as its similar occurrence in the Merseyside dialect. One other feature of the Teesside dialect is that words like Rhyme and

Time are often pronounced Rahm and Tahm.

Thorsday: Geordie for Thursday. Thursday was the day of the Norse and Germanic god called Thor.

Thwaite: A Viking word that occurs in place-names. It means clearing or meadow.

Tyke: An ill-mannered person, or a Yorkshireman, originally signified a dog. It is a word of Viking origin.

Ur sound: In Geordie Dirt, Skirt, Burst and Bird are pronounced Dort, Skort, Borst and Bord, this reflects the old Northern style of speech and has Anglo-Saxon roots.

Waak: In North East dialects this means Walk.

Wath: A Viking word for a ford across a stream or river.

Wearside dialect: A North-East dialect spoken in Sunderland, but having many similarities with surrounding areas of County Durham. It is distinguished from Tyneside in a number of ways. For example 'Make' is pronounced 'Mak' and 'Take' is 'Tak'. The 'oo' sound is often quite distinct so that words like Cool, Fool and School are often pronounced so that they sound like Coowil, Foowil and Skoowil. Compare the almost Germanic pronunciation in Tyneside which uses a short oo sound Cuhl, Fuhl and Skuhl. The dropping of H's at the beginning of a word sometimes occurs in Wearside dialect but does not normally occur in the Tyneside dialect. Wearsiders use traditional pronunciations like 'wrang' for 'wrong' and 'strang' for 'strong'. Phrases like 'get up', and 'sit up' are pronounced 'gerrup' and 'syrup'.

Wife/Wifey: Northern and Scottish word for a woman, whether married or not. It is of Anglo-Saxon origin from 'Wif' or from the Dutch 'Wiif'.

Wor: In Geordie Wor Lass means my wife or girlfriend. Wor is from the Anglo-Saxon word Oor meaning Our. The w has crept into speech naturally.

Worm: A dragon - such as the Lambton Worm or Sockburn Worm. It can be of Scandinavian or Germanic origin.

Wrang: The Northern and original Anglo-Saxon pronunciation of wrong.

Yat: A Yorkshire and Cumbrian pronunication of gate.

Ye: The Anglo-Saxon word for You. It is still used in the North East.

Yem: A Northern word for Home. Of Scandinavian origin. See Hyem.

Yen: In North East dialect means the number one. In Anglo-Saxon it was An, in Frisian Ien in Danish, Norwegian and Swedish En and in Dutch Een.

Yorkshire Dialect: Northern dialect with many variations. It is strongly influenced by the speech of the Angles and Vikings. Generally the old North and East ridings are more closely related than the West Riding dialect. The West Riding dialect displays a number of features distinct from the other Northern dialects. This may be due to Mercian influence. Interestingly only 13% of the place-names in the West Riding are Viking compared to 28% in the North Riding and 40% in the East Riding. Dialect experts often group those parts of the West Riding south of Bradford, Leeds and York with the dialects of the East Midlands rather than those of Northern England. Traditional West Riding pronunciations include Dahn (Down), Mahse (Mouse), Hahse (House), Rahnd (Round). In the North and East Ridings they traditionally use the 'oo' sound.

Timeline

1AD-43AD: Pre-Roman North inhabited by Welsh speaking people.

71AD-122AD: Romans arrive in the North and build Hadrian's Wall.

410AD: Romans abandon Britain.

450AD-550AD: Angles and Saxons invade Britain.

547AD: Angles seize Bamburgh, Kingdom of Bernicia founded.

547AD-600AD: Bernicia and Deira expand.

598AD: Angles defeat Britons at Catterick.

604AD: Bernicia and Deira unite as the Kingdom of Northumbria.

731AD: Bede writes history of England.

793AD: Vikings attack Lindisfarne.

841AD: Norwegians establish Dublin.

866AD: Danes establish settlement at York.

954AD: Eric Bloodaxe, the last Viking King of York is murdered on Stainmore.

918AD: Norsemen from Dublin settle in England.

979AD: Vikings establish Tynwald parliament on the Isle of Man.

1066: Normans invade England.

1069: Seven hundred Normans massacred in Durham City.

Circa 1100-1400: Surnames begin to develop.

1139-1157: North East England is part of Scotland.

Circa 1150-1500: English spoken in this period is called Middle English.

1190: Jews massacred in York.

1207: Liverpool receives a town charter.

1213: Port of Hull established by the King.

1266: Norwegians sell Isle of Man to Scotland.

1301: Manchester receives a town charter.

1322: Fulling Mill recorded at Manchester.

1400-1603: Height of Border Reiving activity.

1600-1800: Railways developing in colliery districts of the North.

1700s: Height of Liverpool slave trading activity.

1700-1800: Industry begins to flourish in the North but still largely rural.

1715: First Jacobite rebellion.

1740: Jewish communities in Manchester, Leeds and Liverpool.

1745: Second Jacobite rebellion.

1746: Battle of Culloden.

1767: Hargreaves invents the Spinning Jenny, improving textile production.

1781: First Jewish settlement in the North East at Sunderland.

1789: Manchester's population is 50,000.

1801: First census. There is a famine in Ireland.

1801: Manchester has a population of 70,000.

1816: Leeds linked to Liverpool by canal.

1825-1840: Railway Age begins, towns begin to expand.

1825: Around 100,000 Irish people live in Lancashire.

1829: Middlesbrough is still a farm.

1845: Irish potato famine. Many Irish seek work in Northern England.

1847: Hong Kong under British rule.

1857: India comes under British rule.

1868: Suez Canal opens.

1901: End of the Victorian Age.

1914-18: World War One.

1939-1945: World War Two.

1947: Division of India.

Further Reading

A.H.Smith, *Place Names of the East Riding* (English Place-Name Society, Cambridge University Press, 1937).

A.H.Smith, *Place Names of the North Riding* (English Place-Name Society, Cambridge University Press, 1928).

A.Mawer, *Place Names of Northumberland and Durham* (Cambridge University Press, 1920).

Arnold Kellett, *Basic Broad Yorkshire*: (Arnold Kellett, 1992).

Arnold Kellett, *Yorkshire Dictionary* (Smith Settle, Otley, 1994).

Bill Griffiths, *North East Dialect Survey and Word List* (Centre for Northern Studies, University of Northumbria, 1999).

Bill Griffiths, *North East Dialect The Texts* (Centre for Northern Studies, University of Northumbria, 2000).

John Morris, General Editor *Boldon Book (1183):* (Phillimore, 1983).

Cecil Geesom, *Northumberland and Durham Word Book* (Harold Hill, Newcastle upon Tyne, 1969).

Charles Barber, *The English Language A Historical Introduction* (Cambridge University Press, 1993).

Colin D. Rogers, *The Surname Detective* (Manchester University Press, 1995).

D.Hey, *Yorkshire from 1000 AD* (Longman, 1986).

D.W.Rollinson, *History of Cumberland and Westmorland*(Phillimore, Chichester, 1978).

David Crystal, *Cambridge Encyclopedia of the English Language* (Cambridge University Press, 1995).

David Simpson, *Corners of Durham* (North Pennine Publishing, 1992).

David Simpson, *Durham Millennium* (The Northern Echo, 1995).

David Simpson, *Hadrian's Vale and Geordieland* (North Pennine Publishing, 1991).

David Simpson, *Prince Bishop Country* (North Pennine Publishing, 1991).

David Simpson, *Shore of the Saints* (North Pennine Publishing, 1991).

David Simpson, *Steel River* (The Northern Echo, 1996).

David Simpson, *The Border County* (North Pennine Publishing, 1991).

David Simpson, *The Millennium History of North East England* (leighton, 1999).

David Simpson, *Vale of the Vikings, the River Tees* (North Pennine Publishing, 1991).

John Morris, General Editor, *Domesday Book Yorkshire (1086)* (Phillimore, 1983).

Douglas Pocock and Roger Norris, *History of County. Durham* (Phillimore, Chichester, 1990).

E.Royle, *Modern Britain: A Social History 1750-1987* (Arnold, 1987).

Ellert Ekwall, *The Concise Oxford Dictionary of English Place Names*, reprint of 4th edn published 1960 (Oxford University Press, 1987).

F.B.Singleton and S.Rawnsley, *History of Yorkshire* (Phillimore, Chichester 1986).

F.McDonald and J.Cresswell, *Guinness Book of British Place Names* (Guinness Publishing, 1993).

Frank Musgrove, *The North of England, A History from Roman Times to the Present* (Basil Blackwell, Oxford, 1990).

Hugh Heinrick, *A Survey of the Irish in England* (1872), Edited by Alan O'Day (The Hambledon Press, 1990).

J.D.A Widdowson and Clive Upton, *Oxford Atlas of English Dialects* (Oxford University Press, 1996).

J.Haywood, Penguin *Historical Atlas of the Vikings* (Penguin Books, 1995)

J.J.Bagley, *History of Lancashire*, 6th edn first published 1976 (Phillimore, Chichester, 1982 reprint).

John Waddington Feather, *Yorkshire Dialect*, 2nd edn (Dalesman, 1991).

Leslie W.Hepple, *History of Northumberland & Newcastle upon Tyne* (Phillimore, Chichester, 1976).

Martyn Wakelin, *Discovering English Dialects*, 4th edn (Shire Publications, Buckinghamshire, 1994).

N.Higham, *The Northern Counties to AD 1000* (Longman Group Ltd, 1986).

Nick Higham, *The Kingdom of Northumbria* (Alan Sutton Publishing, 1993).

Norman McCord and Richard Thompson, *The Northern Counties from AD 1000* (Addison Wesley Longman, 1998).

P.Cavill, S.Harding, J.Jesch, *Wirral and its Viking Heritage* (English Place-Name Society, Nottingham, 2000).

P.H Reaney and R.M.Wilson, *A Dictionary of English Surnames* 3rd edn, first published 1958 (Oxford University Press, 1995).

Peter Aughton, *Liverpool, a People's History* (Carnegie Publishing, 1993).

Peter Metcalfe, *Place Names of the Yorkshire Dales* (North Yorkshire Marketing, Otley, 1992).

Peter Wright, *Cumbrian Chat* (Dalesman, 1995).

Peter Wright, *Yorkshireman's Dictionary* (Dalesman, 1991).

R.O. Heslop, *Northumbrian Words*

Ruth-Ann Harris, *The Nearest Place that Wasn't Ireland: 19th century Irish labour migration* (Athens, USA, 1994).

Robert Gambles, *Lake District Place Names* (Dalesman, 1980).

S.I.Martin, *Britain's Slave Trade* 2nd edn (Channel 4 Books, 1999).

Stephen Harding, *Ingimund's Saga, Norwegian Wirral*, foreword by Magnus Magnusson K.B.E (Countyvise, Birkenhead, 2000).

Steven Fielding, *Class and Ethnicity: Irish Catholics in England 1880-1939* (Buckingham, 1993).

Tom McArthur, Editor, *The Oxford Companion to the English Language* (Oxford University Press, 1998).

V.Watts, *A Dictionary of County Durham Place-Names* (English Place-Name Society, Nottingham 2002).

W.G.Hoskins, *Local History in England*, 3rd edn (Longman, 1984).

W.J.Lowe, *The Irish in Mid Victorian Lancashire, The Shaping of a Working Class Community* (Peter Lang, New York, 1989).

Websites and Electronic Resources

1881 British Census and National Index on CD Rom (Church of Jesus Christ of Latter Day Saints, 1999).

Black Britannica
www.blackbritannica.co.uk

Commission for Racial Equality
www.cre.gov.uk

History of Islam in the UK
www.bbc.co.uk

Jewish settlements in the North East
www.northeastjewish.org.uk

Liverpool and the slave Trade
www.bbc.co.uk/liverpool

The Scottish Archive Network
www.scan.org.uk

Public Records Office www.pro.gov.uk

I am greatly indebted to Mr Vic Woods of Yearby near Redcar for sharing his knowledge and enthusiasm for the origins of Northern England.

David Simpson.

Index